MW01181796

ISBN: 9781313285186

Published by:
HardPress Publishing
8345 NW 66TH ST #2561
MIAMI FL 33166-2626

Email: info@hardpress.net
Web: http://www.hardpress.net

LEGENDS AND TALES OF THE
HARZ MOUNTAINS.

Legends and Tales

OF THE

Harz Mountains,

NORTH GERMANY.

<hr>

MRS. MARIA ELISE T. T. LAUDER,

Author of "Evergreen Leaves; or, Toofie in Europe."

SECOND EDITION.

TORONTO:

WILLIAM BRIGGS, 78 & 80 KING ST. EAST.

C. W. COATES, Montreal, Que.   S. F. HUESTIS, Halifax, N.S.

London: HODDER & STOUGHTON, 27 Paternoster Row.

1885.

Dedicated

(BY SPECIAL PERMISSION)

TO HER MAJESTY

MARGHERITA,

QUEEN OF ITALY.

PREFACE.

It was during my first summer visit to the Harz Mountains that the idea occurred to me of making a collection of the most interesting of the legends of this charming district. This appeared to me all the more desirable, since no such collection peculiar to this mountain range exists in English.

I wrote on the subject to the celebrated German author Gustav Freytag, unfolding my scheme, which he highly approved, and he very kindly rendered me valuable assistance by naming some of the books—and these were not a few—which it might be needful to study, and the libraries where they would be found.

From a vast mass—up into the thousands—of *Sagen*, or legends and traditions, I chose the most interesting, *giving them as I found them*, when they were only pure translations.

Some of the stories are, however, original, being founded on some legend.

No mountainous district of Germany is, perhaps, so rich in legendary lore as this most northern chain. Every ruin of castle or *Kloster*, every mountain stream, is haunted by the Fairies, Gnomes, Cobolds, and Dwarfs, who guard hidden treasures, and watch over the destinies of mankind, and in its mountain recesses, captive princesses and fair maidens are supposed to sigh for freedom, or the dead Kaiser, the old Redbeard, awaits, surrounded with royal magnificence, the day of Germany's greatest power.

There are numerous wild tales told of the sandstone mountain, the Regenstein or Reinstein, from the times of the invading Huns, down to later days, and its summit commands a wide prospect over mountain and plain.

The immortal German poet Goethe, has rendered the witch-haunted Brocken forever famous through his master-poem "Faust." What visitor to its fog-crowned summit has not shaken hands with the *Spectre* of the Brocken? Down its massive slopes the limpid river Ilse tosses itself over huge, moss-grown granite boulders, forming hundreds of tiny water-falls. It was while rambling in this lovely vale the little poem "Alone," was written, which I have put into the mouth of my personal friend, the Countess von Omnesky, the mother of the little Tatjana.

The Harz is the birth-place of the " Wild Hunter," of the " Wild Army " of South Germany, of the Gold Crown, and of the noble Brünhilda. The view from the top of the granite mountain, the Hexentanzplatz, to the distant Brocken in clear weather, and across to that mass of granite, the Rosstrappe, the swift Bode leaping over huge blocks of fallen granite between, and a thousand feet below, is one of the finest in these mountains. This spot is the scene of the legend of Brünhilda.

On the summit of the Rosstrappe is a giant horse-hoof, hewn in the solid granite, measuring nearly three feet. How this mark came there is a mystery ; but it is supposed that it was hewn by the Druid priests. In the Scandinavian mythology Wodan's white steed was worshipped as well as the god himself.

When Charlemagne, in the eighth century, compelled the people of this district to embrace Christianity (by fire and sword) the wild mountaineers are supposed to have fled before his victorious forces, and to have entrenched themselves on the Rosstrappe, where traces of their rude fortifications may still be seen. They had no white steed to worship in this retreat, hence probably, the priests cut this rut of a horse-hoof, and invented the story of Brünhilda and the Giant's White Horse, in order to impress the people with the mighty power of the Thunder-god, and prevent them from entertaining any sympathy for the new religion.

From this point the echoes of the horn through the mountains are indescribably beautiful.

In the charming *Ilsenthal*, or valley of the Ilse, we found the home of the fascinating Princess Ilse, who is fabled to dwell in unearthly splendor in the mountain, the Ilsenstein, at the foot of which the transformed offenders of the Princess sigh and moan in the form of fir-trees. Should you, my dear reader, ever enjoy their refreshing shade, may Princess Ilse be as gracious to you as she was to me, and may your *Dream under Princess Ilse's Firs* prove still more pleasant than mine.

TOOFIE LAUDER.

CONTENTS.

Contents.

LEGENDS AND TALES.

Legend of the Rosstrappe.*

AGES ago there ruled a king in Bohemia whose castle stood on a lofty mountain, where the thunder and the eagle found a home.

This king had a daughter, the golden-haired Brunhilda, the fame of whose marvellous beauty was spread far and wide.

Mighty rulers and the sons of kings sought the hand of the lovely royal maiden, and among the numerous wooers came the son of the king of the Harz, who won her heart; and after the lovers had sworn everlasting fidelity, the Harz† Prince returned to his father to announce his betrothal and make arrangements for the nuptials.

After his departure, there arrived a new suitor for Brunhilda's hand, whom her father feared to reject. This was one of those terrible giants who inhabited North Europe. They were invincible, and wherever they appeared, all yielded with terror to their might.

Ross, a steed; *Trappe*, a footprint.　　†Harz or Hartz.

This dreadful lover brought the Princess costly gifts of gold, amber, and precious stones. The father, after three days' *Bedenkzeit** promises the Giant his daughter.

Brunhilda throws herself horrified on her knees before her father, weeping and tearing her hair; but the king, though moved with pity, assures her the Giant has power to destroy him and his kingdom.

From this hour Brunhilda appeared composed. She neither wept nor complained, but met her destined bridegroom with a solemn dignity. Of a truly kingly character, she constrained her agony to silence, but hoped ever for deliverance through the return of her Harz lover; still he came not.

Now the Giant had two steeds—giant steeds—one white as the snows of the Northland, his eyes shining like stars; the other, the Giant's body-horse, black as the night, with eyes like the lightning, at whose running his hoofs resounded like thunder, and the earth trembled and shook. Both these steeds seemed in the chase to overtake the storm, and keep time with the lightning.

Brunhilda saw these giant steeds, and the thought of flight occurred to her.

Was success possible? She had never mounted the snowy steed.

Great was the Giant's joy when Brunhilda begged to ride with him. She mounted daily the terrible

Bedenkzeit, time for consideration.

animal, and soon could ride a race with the Giant on the mountains.

At last the evening before the nuptials arrived, and Brunhilda, having arrayed herself in white robes, a golden crown, and a long white veil floating behind her, and the amber and diamonds, the Giant's gifts, welcomed the numerous guests who thronged the royal palace, and looked lovingly upon the Giant Bräutigam,* who was overwhelmed with an unheard-of bliss at the lovely vision.

At length the Princess rose and retired, the Giant remained to drink of the costly wines. Suddenly he heard the snorting and stamping of his war-steeds! He sprang up and looked down into the courtyard.

There sat Brunhilda in her glittering robes, the golden crown still upon her head, her white veil and golden hair fluttering in the wind, in her fearless courage and queenly beauty, upon the snowy steed before the open gates.

At sight of him she let loose her reins, and the mighty steed shot forth, swift as the storm-wind, like a streak of light, into the darkness of the night.

The Giant uttered a cry of fury that shook the castle to its foundations, seized his battle-axe, and mounted his war-horse, crying: "If she flee to the Nidhöggar † in the Schlangengrund ‡ I will bring her hence!"

* *Bräutigam*, bridegroom. Used only during the engagement.
† *Nidhöggar*, the dragon in the old German water-hell.
‡ *Schlangengrund*, valley of serpents.

And now begins the fearful race. Through meadow and forest, over mountain and ravine, flee the pursuer and pursued, the white steed always in advance, fleeing swift as a meteor through the heavens! behind, the black steed, like a spirit from the eternal darkness.

All through the night lasted the terrible ride. The earth groaned and thundered, the forests trembled, the birds and beasts fled in terror, long streaks of fire swept through the grim darkness, and the snorting of the steeds was like the roar of the Northwind.

At last dawn reflects her rosy blush over mountain and wood. Brunhilda utters a cry of joy and triumph! There before her lies the Harz, her lover's mountain home and future kingdom! That distant peak is the Brocken!

She spurs on her noble steed till she reaches the Hexentanzplatz,* when suddenly he stops, rears, and plunges, and refuses to advance. Before her yawns the terrible, rocky abyss of the Bode Valley, behind she hears the deadly foe advancing, uttering the most dreadful curses!

What shall she do? Forward over the wild abyss? Backward is to fall into the arms of the enemy.

The choice is not difficult. She turns his head to the fearful chasm, and spurs him on.

Like an eagle, the noble animal leaps the yawning abyss, lands safely on the other side, and impressing

---

* *Hexentanzplatz*, witches' dancing-floor.

its giant hoof-print in the granite, sinks exhausted; but the Princess loses her *goldene Krone* in the gulf beneath, the Bode Kessel ! *

The Giant in rage and fury spurs on his dusky steed to leap after her, but falls and is broken on the rocks, and ever since, transformed into a hell-hound, he guards the golden crown in the Bode Kessel.

The Princess, saved, dances for joy, and her foot-prints are still to be seen in the solid granite.

The mountain has ever since been called the Ross-trappe, and the Giant Bodo† gave his name to the valley and river.

The Golden Crown in the Bode Kessel.

" *Seht ihr die alte Lauenburg*
  Hoch auf dem Harze schimmern ?
  Durch Wildniss geht der Weg hindurch
  Zu ihren wüsten Trümmern."

THE legend of the Gold-Krone in the Bode Kessel is connected with a Countess of the Lauenburg.

In the days of the Crusades there dwelt here a fair maiden, the daughter of the Earl von Lauenburg, whose lover, Conrad von Regenstein, was a Crusader.

Instead of his speedy return, came tidings of his fall in the bloody combat. The broken-hearted *Braut* refused all other lovers, and to secure peace and free-

* *Kessel*—gulf.
† *Bodo*—the final o has been corrupted into e, Bode.

dom declared she would bestow her hand only on the knight who could rescue Brunhilda's crown from the fearful gulf, the Bode Kessel.

The news spread through all the plains of Germany, from the North Sea to the Alps, and knights and princes flocked to the banks of the Bodethal to learn the extent of the danger in such an attempt, but no man was even able to approach the brink of the fearful chasm.*

The object of the maiden seemed gained, but, alas! she knew not what anguish destiny had assigned her.

Years had fled, and the Graf† von Lauenburg held a fête in his castle.

Suddenly the notes of the warder's horn resound proclaiming the arrival of a guest.

The young Countess looks out of a Gothic window into the court, turns pale and trembles, as her straining eyes gaze upon the entering knight.

Yes! She is not deceived; that is the figure, the noble bearing of her lost Crusader!

"Conrad! my Conrad!" she cries, and rushes, frantic with joy, into the arms of her returned lover. "Thou dost yet live! Thou liest not in the cold arms of death!"

"I live, am in thy arms!"

---

* It must be remembered that the Bodethal was unapproachable, no path whatever existing, until von Bülow caused the path to be constructed in 1818, past the Rosstrappe to the Devil's Bridge overlooking the Bode Kessel.

† *Graf*—Earl. It is not, however, so high as the title in England.

No word more—a long embrace.

The aged Earl has followed his daughter, and amid their astonishment and joy, Conrad explains how he was severely wounded and taken prisoner, and had not for long years been able to escape.

The father leads the happy pair into the great hall, and announces to the assembled guests the betrothal of his daughter, and an early wedding-day.

Many crowd forward to offer their congratulations; but, in the background of the hall one sees a group of knights with frowning brows.

At last one of the group approaches the Earl in the centre of the hall, and cries: "You are in haste to announce the betrothal and wedding-day. Has the Regensteiner then brought up the Gold-Krone? or are you playing with so many nobles? You are surrounded by many who will demand that the bridegroom fulfil the conditions you yourself have named or they will accuse you of treachery, and renounce your allegiance."

Applause followed this stern address. The Earl, surprised, glanced around the circle and met grim looks and frowning faces.

But Conrad raised high his proud form, struck his sword upon the floor, so that the hall rang with the clang, and cried in a voice of thunder: "Who dares speak of treachery to Graf Lauenburg? Those conditions were not made in jest or scorn; his knightly word is irreproachable. I will undergo the test, and will not lead my beloved home until I have redeemed it.'

Silence and astonishment filled the hall. But the maiden, pale with terror, exclaimed: "What! thou will'st face the Terrible? plunge thyself into certain destruction, and me into fresh despair?"

Conrad assures her the danger is not so great as it appears; that he is protected by an amulet, a cross made from the true cross of the Saviour, that has defended him from ocean perils, and rescued him from the swords and dungeons of the Saracens, and immediately prepares for the perilous rescue.

The day arrived, the Bode was bridged with ice, hundreds of anxious spectators lined the rocks above, the black flag floated from the Lauenburg and the Regenstein.

Extreme unction had been administered in Kloster * Wenthusen, and armed with a dagger for the combat with the transformed Giant Bodo, and an iron chain to bind him, with a look toward heaven, Conrad plunged into the yawning gulf.

The waves closed over him and drew him down into their shimmering bosom.

A long and anxious stillness—then a horrible howl burst forth from the gulf, drowning the roar and hiss of the waterfall, growing every minute louder and more terrible, as if a thousand wolves were engaged in a death-grapple; and the waters rose in mighty billows, as if a storm-wind raged beneath.

* *Kloster,* convent.

Now a ray of sunshine bursts forth, making the colossal rocks glitter like silver towers, and the waterfall like dropping diamonds, and through the pearly foam appears a hand holding the Golden Crown; the howlings become weaker, and the whisper goes round, "He has conquered!" And a loud voice rises above the raging waves, "The Hell-dog lies in chains! The Crown and the beloved are mine!"

Hark! What is that?

The terrible howlings begin afresh, the hand trembles and vanishes with the Gold-Krone, soon all grows fearfully still, drops of blood rise to the surface, then a whole stream—the brave Crusader never returns.

They found the amulet thrown up from the unfathomable deeps, and carried it to the unhappy maiden, who without a tear turned her steps to the holy retreat of Kloster Wenthusen, and was never seen again.

The Seven Springs of Thale.

BETWEEN the red-roofed Thale and Dorf Neinstedt, one sees several low, round hills, here and there overgrown with thorns and thickets, sometimes bare of all vegetation save short grass.

These mounds are graves of primeval days, in which urns and bones have been found.

At the foot of these hills, in a semi-circle, are seven small springs, which unite themselves in one tiny brooklet, over which the train passes.

On the summit of one of these hills once stood seven trees, called the Seven Brothers, of which now no trace remains.

Seven royal brothers came from England to woo the seven daughters of the king of the Harz mountains, the fame of whose beauty had penetrated even to the English court. These princesses were called the Sunbeams of the mountains; and when the English princes arrived in the Felsenburg* of their royal father, they found assembled there princes and nobles from Saxony and Thuringia, Franconia and Bohemia, from the banks of the Danube and the amber coasts of the sea.

But the Sunbeams loved the English princes, and promised to go with them to their father's court.

Then the German wooers were enraged, and said, "Not without combat will we permit these strangers to rob us of the glory of our land."

The brothers seized sword and shield, but the princesses rushed into their arms and hindered the combat.

At midnight, when the full moon shone, each brother, with his affianced bride behind him on his fleet steed, fled toward the rocky shores of England.

Suddenly the affrighted maidens see the glitter of arms in the faint moonlight.

"What is that that glitters below on the plain?" they cry.

"Fear not," said the youths, "'tis the waves of the Bode."

* *Felsenburg*—Rocky fortress.

· "What is that whistling in the forest?"

"The thrushes sing in the shadows of the foliage."

"Do you hear the rustling in the thicket?"

"'Tis but the frightened deer."

"What is that murmur?"

"The spring gushing out of the rocks."

"And that whispering?"

"The wind!"

"You deceive us. Your eyes burn like the lightning; you have seized both sword and shield!"

"Fear not! We are with you; our arm will defend you!"

Out of the thicket rush the concealed rivals; a furious combat follows; the English princes are all slain, their bodies burnt, and the ashes buried.

The princesses returned to their father's castle, but hated the murderers of their English lovers. Every day they went with the dawn to the spot where the brothers lay in their deep slumber, and night found them still there in tears.

Each princess planted a tree by her lover's grave, and when seven moons were passed away, one evening, as they sat by the graves, suddenly they felt a great joy spring up within them: they wiped away their tears, but from them seven springs bubbled up sparkling and clear. Smiling, they gave each other the hand, feeling the hour of reunion was come, and in the morning they were found dead, hand in hand.

Legends of the Teufelsmauer. *

ON the plain stretching away westward from the once imperial Quedlinburg, is the Devil's Wall, which rises in ragged rocks in the most fantastic shapes and forms, sometimes a hundred feet in height, mostly bare, but nearer to Blankenburg adorned with foliage.

This is the backbone of a mountain chain once extending from Blankenburg to Ballenstedt, which has been mostly washed away by the tempests of untold ages.

These rocks are a firm sandstone with a vein of iron, containing impressions of fossils, shells, and plants, and are sometimes in such forms as to resemble the ruins of castles or human figures.

These rent and torn rocks could not fail to possess their legends.

In the time of Charlemagne there lived in Blanka a maiden called Thusnelda.† The report of her charms attracted the attention of the brave Egbert, who had built on the Klus,‡ near Halberstadt, a strong castle. He won her affections, of course.

Just at this period the doctrines of the Christian faith had penetrated into the Harz; Egbert had become a convert, and had won Thusnelda also for the new faith.

But the lovers were betrayed to Thusnelda's father,

---

* *Teufel*—the devil ; *Mauer*—a wall.   † *Thusnelda* —pronounced Toognelda.   ‡ *Klus*—pronounced Kloos.

the wild and savage Luitprand, and he, in fury, having promised her to a companion in arms, shut her up in a gloomy room, deaf to all her entreaties, and laid in wait for Egbert; but Egbert assembled all the Christian knights of the neighbourhood, and set off in the night to storm Luitprand's castle.

Suddenly a wall of rock rose before them, and they were obliged to wait till morning, when lo! as far as they could see, only this formidable barrier that blocked up their way.

Egbert encouraged his Braves to climb it ; but when half way up, the giant rocks fell upon them and crushed every daring knight to atoms.

This wall the devil had built to prevent the spread of the new faith.

The other legend says the devil wished to divide with Christ the empire of the world, and therefore began this wall as the border between the two kingdoms ; but the work was not finished at the time agreed upon by the contracting parties, and the contract was broken. The devil, in wrath at having laboured so much for nought, broke in pieces his partly-built defence.

There is a tradition that the holy Vehm,* or Fehm, formerly held her court also in the Teufelsmauer, not far from the majestic Reinstein.

This celebrated tribunal had its origin in West-

---

* *Vehm*, or *Fehm*, old German for punishment. *Vehm*—pronounced Vame ; *Fehm*—pronounced Fame.

phalia, the land of the Red Earth, and was one of
the most remarkable institutions of the middle ages.

The Fehm is said to have been instituted by
Charlemagne to prevent Saxony, which had been
forced by his arms to embrace Christianity, from
returning to Paganism. Others claim for it a much
greater antiquity.*

The Wunderstein.

THE vast plain north of the Harz mountains has
been the scene of countless knightly feuds and
battles.

In 1115 the battle of Welfsholz—not far from the
village of Warnstedt, nestling in the shadow of the
Devil's Wall—was fought between the Kaiser and the
allied princes of Saxony, in which the imperial forces
were routed. There is a legend that the battle was lost
through the Count von Mannsfeld,† who seeing his
men flee, exclaimed, placing his hand on a rock at his
side, "This rock shall turn into wax before I move
from the spot!" when immediately the soft wax
yielded to the pressure, and took the print of his hand,
and he fled in terror and fell under the Saxon swords.

There is another version of the story.

Before the battle, the Earl von Mannsfeld called his
men in a circle around him, and addressed them thus:
"My friends! fear not because the enemy outnumbers

* See "History of the Fehm Tribunal; or, Secret History of
Westphalia." By Fr. P. Usener. Frankfort, 1832.
† Mannsfeld or Mansfeld.

us; let the rebels come, we will be•their death-angel, for, listen all of you, and doubt not of victory, for so sure as my hand presses itself into this rock as if it were dough, so sure will the victory rest with our flag as long as I fight with you."

And before a thousand eager eyes he thrust his hand into the stone, leaving a deep rut.

Enthusiasm inspired the souls of the soldiers at the sight, and shouts of joy went through the ranks.

It is a fact that the brave Mannsfeld, impatient of victory, rushed on before his men and fell.

In the old Kloster of Wenthusen in Dorf Thale—pronounced Talé—is still preserved a mysterious Wonderstone, which is said to protect the estate and family from misfortune. By some mishap this stone was once carried off, and disaster followed disaster till it was brought back.

Charlotte of Blankenburg, Princess of Wolfenbüttel.

ON the north side of the Harz mountains lies the town of Blankenburg, the origin of which is long prior to the time of Charlemagne, probably during that of the Sassen. It existed during the stone and bronze age, as has been proved by the discovery of warlike implements which have been dug up in the neighbourhood.

On a low mountain above the town stands Blankenburg* Schloss, white and shining in the summer's

* *Blankenburg*, the shining castle.

sun, and looks out on the vast plain, the Devil's Wall,
and the mountains.   Its long suites of bright and
home-like apartments are adorned with many costly
works of art, the most precious of which being the
wondrously carved ivory crucifix in the chapel, by
Michael Angelo.   With all this we have at present
nothing to do, but rather with the singular destiny of
a lady who was born here, whose portrait hangs in the
drawing and billiard room.

Duke Ludwig Rudolph, second son of Duke Anton
Ulrick of Brunswick, was presented by his father with
the Earldom of Blankenburg.   He lived with his wife,
Princess Christine Louise von Oettingen, thirty years
in Schloss Blankenburg.

They were the parents of three princesses, noted as
well for goodness of heart as for grace and beauty.
The eldest was Elizabeth Christine, born in 1691.
The second, Charlotte Christiane Sophie, was a year
younger.   The youngest, Antoinette Amalie, was born
in 1696.

The eldest, Elizabeth, was chosen at the age of
thirteen, by Kaiser Leopold, as consort of his son Carl
III., King of Spain, later Carl VI. of Germany.   She
was the mother of the great Maria Theresa.   The
young princess went over to the Romish faith, and
met her royal bridegroom in Barcelona, where they
were married.   In consequence of this alliance with
the Imperial family, the Earldom was raised to a
Principality by Joseph I.   It now belongs to the
Duchy of Brunswick.

The second, Princess Charlotte, was chosen by the Czar, Peter the Great, who spent some time here, as consort for his son and throne-heir, Alexis.

The third, Antoinette, the loveliest of the three sisters, married Duke Ferdinand Albert of Brunswick-Bevern. She is the ancestress of the now reigning family of Brunswick. *

It is the history of the second sister, Princess Charlotte, with which we have to do. Her marriage with the Czarewitch Alexis took place in 1711, in the great hall in Torgau.

The savage, vulgar Prince had made his character still more degraded by a dissipated life. An unconquerable aversion to the amiable and refined Princess led him to the horrible decision of poisoning her. He made three attempts, all of which failed.

The inhuman treatment of this monster increased daily, and no courtier dared to defend the unhappy Princess against his brutality. He so far forgot his manhood as frequently to strike, and even kick her.

At length, one day, the Czar and Catherine being on a distant journey, Alexis rushed into Charlotte's presence, made the most brutal demands, struck her with his fists, kicked her repeatedly, and left her lying insensible.

Directly after this revolting scene the raging monster set off on a journey, without troubling himself to

* Since this was written this line has become extinct, by the demise of the late Duke of Brunswick.

3

learn the result of his barbarous and fiendish cruelty. A premature birth was the result.

But now the friends of the Princess united for her rescue; the opportunity was too favourable to let slip.

A courier was despatched to the Czar, and also to Alexis, with the news of Charlotte's sudden death. In his terror of the Czar, Alexis ordered an immediate interment. The funeral followed as had been commanded, but the coffin contained only a wooden doll.

While all the courts of Europe put on mourning, and the father wept for his untimely loss, and caused a commemorative coin to be struck, Charlotte, with the aid of confidential friends, especially the famous Aurora von Königsmark, escaped, weak and ill, from her palace. With gold and jewels, and as much money as could be commanded in the hurry, the Princess left St. Petersburg with a single *femme de chambre* and a faithful man-servant, reached Paris unrecognized, sailed for America, and lived many years in Louisiana.

Here she made the acquaintance of the Chevalier d'Aubert—or d'Auban—who had been in St. Petersburg. One day, when alone with Charlotte, he fell on his knees and confessed his recognition of her.

The Princess took from him the most solemn promise of the strictest secrecy.

Not long after, the papers brought the news of the tragical end of Alexis, the probability of his having been beheaded.

Charlotte, however, resolved to remain as dead. The death of her devoted man-servant, who had been of such service, caused her many tears, and d'Aubert devoted himself to her, became her chief prop and stay, and at length the royal widow rewarded him with her hand.

D'Aubert finally fell ill, and they returned to his native France, where his recovery was her reward.

They were in the habit of walking in the gardens of the Tuileries. One day, sitting there conversing in German, chance led the celebrated Marshal Moritz* von Saxony past them. Surprised to hear his mother tongue so purely spoken by Americans, as he imagined, he approached them, addressed the lady, started, and instantly recognized the Princess Charlotte of Blankenburg, whom he had long years reckoned among the dead.

Madame d'Aubert conjured him not to betray her secret, told him her story, and how it had been chiefly through his mother she had succeeded in escaping from Russia.

Delighted at the double discovery, Moritz promised to keep the secret three months, at the expiration of which time he declared it to be his duty to communicate the fact to the King of France, Louis XV.

D'Aubert being recovered, they sailed for l'île Bourbon. At the end of three months Moritz revealed the secret to the French sovereign, and the governor of

* Moritz von Saxony was a son of Augustus the Strong of Saxony King of Poland.

the island of Bourbon received forthwith the command to treat Madame d'Aubert with royal honours. The King wrote to Maria Theresa, acquainting her with the fabulous story of her niece. The Empress wrote to Madame d'Aubert, beseeching her to leave her husband and repair to the Austrian Court. This the Princess refused to do, and remained on the island till d'Aubert's death, in 1754. After the death of both husband and daughter, she returned to Paris, settled the affairs of her husband, and retired to Brussels, where she received an annual pension from the Austrian Empress. Charlotte lived a retired life, no one but the now aged waiting-woman who had fled with her having the remotest idea of her high rank and astounding fate. Charlotte died in 1770.

The portraits of the three sisters and the great Maria Theresa hang in Blankenburg Schloss.

The Grave Under the Lindens Near Blankenburg.

" Sie ruhen bei einander kühl,
Waldvöglein sangen droben,
Grün Laub herunter fiel."

MANY hundred years ago there lived a rich Earl in the Unterharz, who was once sized with a severe illness ; he made a vow that if he should recover, he would consecrate his daughter to a convent life.

He recovered, and the young Countess in the first bloom of her youth, entered the convent north of and near Blankenburg, where now two large lindens stand close by the bleaching-place.

The maiden obeyed her father's command with a heavy heart, for a young knight contested with heaven his claim on the bride; and however much the novice knelt before the altar in burning tears and hand-wringing, and besought heavenly aid in renouncing all she had hitherto held dear, still her thoughts would wander beyond the dark convent walls and lonely cell to her lover. *Nobis pacem* only awakened a more bitter pain, and the *Ave*, the *Laudamus*, the *Gloria*, and all the Penitential Psalms only called up his image before her soul.

Lindor was not less unhappy; in vain he sought to approach his *Braut*, wandered round and round the convent walls, climbed the trees, and watched to catch a glimpse of her, all in vain. The Abbess knew of the love of the young novice, and watched her with Argus-eyes, not out of holy zeal, for the convent had long been ill-renowned for the impure life of its inmates, but out of hatred to the maiden whose father she had loved, but with an unrequited affection. She rejoiced in the deep sorrow of the daughter of the now hated Earl, whose pure, pious, unsoiled character enraged her still more, in striking contrast to her own depravity and corruption. One day the sorrowing novice, un-happily, by accident discovered how unworthily the Abbess filled her sacred office, and how great the im-morality of the nuns had become, and the Abbess, to render Lina powerless to injure her, resolved to destroy her.

She called together those nuns who were in her full confidence, represented to them how they had to fear betrayal from the novice Lina, and to defend themselves they must destroy her.

This would be most easily accomplished by permitting a meeting with her lover after she had assumed the veil, surprise her, accuse her of breaking her vow, and then wall her up alive.

The reprobates approved of this diabolical plan, and as soon as Lina's novitiate was ended, and she had taken the final vows, they embraced the first opportunity, when Lindor was seen in the convent grounds, by giving Lina permission to walk in the garden.

It was a sultry Saturday evening, the sun had set, and had left, instead of a golden twilight, only a grey, cloudy veil, which, increased by the mountain mists, spread gradually over the entire heavens, proclaiming a coming thunder-storm.

Lina, although she had long languished for fresh air, found no relief. She glanced toward heaven, but both moon and stars were hidden behind the dark clouds; the flowers hung sadly their drooping heads, as if in sympathy with the maiden doomed to a convent life. She sat down much shaken on a seat of turf shaded by two lindens, and the tears streamed from her eyes. Suddenly she felt herself embraced. A cry of delighted surprise escaped her, for it was Lindor, her beloved. All sorrow and pain were forgotten in the bliss of the meeting, and Lindor kissed the tears from her burning cheeks.

A blissful moment—the lovers embraced each other; then came a feeling of duty, of assumed vows, before the soul of the bride of heaven, like a fiend of darkness. She tore herself from his arms.

"Lindor! Lindor!" she moaned, "I am lost to thee; our embrace is sin! O God! God of Love! have mercy on the sinner! Lindor! Lindor! have thou also pity! Leave me."

"Leave thee! Nevermore!" cried passionately the youth; "now thou art mine for ever. Thou shalt flee with me, and no power on earth shall tear thee from me. Thou art mine—mine till death!"

"And my oath," cried Lina; "the oath I have taken?"

"Lindor turned pale. "So thou hast already taken the vows—art no longer novice? Art irrevocably chained to the convent?" he cried in horror, for even love started back from the gulf that such an oath had made between them, opposing their union. "Then I am lost, my life-happiness is annihilated!"

"And mine too!" sobbed Lina in his arms.

"Or wilt thou flee with me? We will hide ourselves far from our native land, where no searcher can find us, and undisturbed we will be happy."

But Lina refused. "My oath! my oath! would it leave us peace? Would I not draw down thy soul to perdition ?   See, my anguish will soon be over, and I will wait for thee above.   Give me up for this life, that God may grant us a blessed future, Lindor."

He gazed on the ground, and was silent.   At last he gave her the hand.   "Let it be so," he said, struggling for firmness.   "Thou art still mine; if not here, there above."

Meanwhile the storm-clouds had blackened, and a loud clap of thunder rolled over the heads of the parting lovers.   Both looked up, but did not see the Abbess, who was watching them for their destruction.

"Now let us part for this life," said Lina, who felt her soul elevated and strengthened.

"Must it be so ?   Must I lose thee when I have just found thee ?"

As they gave each other a parting embrace, Lina could not tear herself from her lover's arms, and cried, " O Father in heaven ! give me strength in this parting hour, and forgive me if my love is sin ; but if it is not sin, bless our union."

" Bless our union !" repeated Lindor.   At this moment the Abbess, with her nuns, came forward, when lo ! a flash of lightning lit up the darkness ; the lovers stood in a sea of dazzling light.   It seemed to them they saw heaven open.   Arm-in-arm, struck by the stroke, they sank lifeless to the ground.   Almost unhurt in appearance, they found them under the lindens, heavenly joy painted on their faces, and there they made their grave.

The terrified Abbess had scarcely sprung back into the convent when a stream of fire, after a terrific thunder-clap, dashed the building to ruins, out of which arose a pillar of dust and flame.

Only a few of the nuns were rescued. The Abbess and her plotting nuns were found awfully disfigured; and now, it is said, the Abbess appears in form of a serpent every seven years near the grave under the Linden.

Legends of the Regenstein.

WHO that has visited the romantic Harz has not climbed the lordly sandstone mountain, the Reinstein, wondered at its vast chambers hewn in the solid rock, and gazed in silent rapture on a prospect more beautiful than that from the Brocken?

In the year 479, according to the chroniclers, the sharp contest between the tribes of Thuringia and the Sassen* took place for the possession of the Harz mountains. Melverich, King of Thuringia, with his army, thirsting for war, crossed the mountains to repulse the Sassen then dwelling on the north borders of the Harz.

Near Wernigerode a bloody battle was fought, in which the Thuringians were defeated, and five thousand left dead on the field.

Perhaps the Hun stones still standing between Heimburg and Benzingerode have reference to this

* Saxons.

fiery collision, and the ancient burial-places discovered in the vicinity were the graves of those fallen in this contest.

After the battle the Sassen recognized the fact that to their leader, Hatebolt, they owed the victory, and to prove their gratitude they offered to build him a castle on the north borders of the Harz, in any spot he might choose. So Hatebolt rode till he came to a stone mountain, which was, as if by nature, formed for a stronghold. It rose rugged and steep from the sandy heath to a mighty rock, and formed a row of impassable cliffs, the western summits of which widened into a table-land sufficiently broad for the site of a castle.

And Hatebolt pointed to the row of rocks, and cried, in the language of the Sassen, " On this Regen-stein* my Burg shall stand !"

That is the fortress whose magnificent position still delights us, at whose ruins we gaze in amazement, in whose halls and chambers, almost entirely hewn in the rocks, we see the work of a far-distant time, when comfort and luxury were unknown in this region.

From these grey ruins, from the grim vaults, the half-fallen tower, and the deep dungeon, breathes the spirit of the past, and whispers many a legendary note in the ear. Is it the mysterious Devil's Hole in an ancient vault, with the date 1090, near which house spectres, whose employment it is ever to fill this four

* *Regenstein*, or *Reinstein*, row of rocks.

feet deep and wide hole with stones; or the opening in one of the larger rock walls, which proclaims a conquest of the castle; or the ruinated chapel, with its tiny Gothic door and two windows, and the aumbry still in the wall at the right on entering; the over-grown moat to the east and south; the arched entrance, the many half-broken flights of stone steps? All this has an untold mystic charm.

The opening in the wall was made at a seizure of the castle, which tradition tells us was accomplished by stratagem.

The besiegers had lain long before the stronghold in vain, had stormed the walls and the stronger rocks without success, and finally, evidently convinced that the fortress was impregnable, had raised the siege. And now there were feasting and joy, and the Earl von Regenstein commanded the best wine to be brought. But for security, in case of another attack, he resolved to lay in fresh provisions, and accordingly sent a messenger to the surrounding villages with an order to the people forthwith to bring the needful supplies.

In a short time a troop of peasants, men and women, appeared, half-bent from the weight of baskets on their backs, and tubs of butter and cheese under the arm. The great gates were opened, the drawbridge lowered, and the troop entered. But once inside, they threw baskets and tubs to the winds, seized their arms, drove back the surprised guard, and at the same time a party in ambush rushed over the drawbridge. They cut down all that opposed them, but the Earl was nowhere to be found. When he saw himself out-witted, and that all opposition was useless, and every issue from the fortress in possession of the enemy, he caused himself to be sewed up in a bed, and let down on the north and perpendicular side of the rocks with ropes. The opening is still shown in one of the rocky chambers through which he is said to have escaped.

Another legend is connected with the dungeon, which is hewn deep down in the rocks. A captured maiden had been imprisoned here, and had sat long in the darkness of constant night, hearing no sound save that of the raging storms that beat against the rocks. Escape was impossible. One day she lay on her bed of straw, and sought comfort in fervent prayer. And there dawned a distant hope in her mind. She listened to the storm, and heard the hail beat against the rock walls of the dungeon, hence they must be thin. Might she perhaps break through the rocks? They are only very porous sandstone. It is a bold thought, no sooner awakened in her mind than put in execution. She used the ring of the dungeon to break away bits of the rock, and worked many moons till she had an opening large enough to creep through. But what was her despair to find she stood on a dizzy height, and the fearful depth yawned beneath her. Still she did not hesitate, but began climbing down the smooth rocks, which offered only here and there a crevice to her aid. But Tradition, who believeth all things and never faileth, says she reached the foot of the mountain and her father's castle in safety.

Another legend relates how a wealthy countryman had lent an Earl von Regenstein a large sum of money, but when he came to demand payment was repulsed with scorn and derision. Soon after the Earl did not return from a predatory excursion, and many singular reports were circulated concerning his death. The countryman hoped for payment from the Earl's heir, but he treated him more roughly than his predecessor had done. The creditor, on his way home, heard suddenly a loud noise like the crackling of flames. He looked around and saw a cleft in the mountain, from which issued smoke. He went and looked in. It was the mouth of a cave, in the deeps of which pitch and sulphur flames with loud hissing enveloped each other, and in the midst of this fire-gulf he saw a human form, over which the flames swept without consuming it, and which sought, wailing and moaning, to escape, but fell ever back into the boiling heat, with wringing of hands and tearing of hair.

He soon recognized the Earl, who after some minutes saw the creditor whom he had cheated at the entrance to the cave, and broke out in lamentations and entreaties.

" Oh ! see how I must suffer for my injustice. Have pity on my anguish, forgive my crime. Take my signet ring, go to my successor, tell him what you have seen, warn him not to act as I have done, and to pay my debt, that I may escape from this bed of flames."

The countryman hastened to fulfil the commission, showing the signet ring. He was at once paid with heavy interest, and the castle chaplain received orders to read a mass for the suffering soul.

On his way home the countryman looked again into the cave, but nothing more was to be seen either of the flames or the guilty Earl.

The Spectre Maiden of the Regenstein still haunts the ruins.

How solemnly the old ruinated fortress looks down upon the plain bathed in the rich lights of sunset And around the walls and the tower sighs a spirit and sighs the storm.

Let thy stay there be short and cautious, for the ruins are haunted by night. A maiden form rises from the dark vault, and wanders to the tower, and to the great gates, and an innocent countenance smiles upon thee. Guard thyself well, O wanderer; gaze not so deep in the mournful eyes; it is the Spectre Maiden. She bows to thee in graceful greeting, she offers thee the full lips to kiss, she beckons, she spreads out the arms. Oh, follow her not ! Her breath is poison ! If thou grant her the kiss, thou wilt fall an irrecoverable prey to death. Her greeting, her beckon are not for thee ; she waits here for her lover.

As Crusader, he marched to the Holy Sepulchre. She is gazing after him from the tower 'waiting for his return by the broken drawbridge, and wanders ever in search of him.

If she meet thee, she will fancy thou art her fallen hero-lover. If thou dost follow when she beckons, she will draw thee into an open grave with ice-cold arms.

> Oh! guard thyself well when in her sight,
> For she haunts the Regenstein by night!

The Lost Sketch-Book of the Regenstein Chapel.

THE Baronin von Felsen had led her young English friend, May Rosenmore, through the ruins of Schloss Regenstein, the authentic history of which begins with Kaiser Henry the Fowler, till at last they wandered to the tiny roofless chapel.

As May entered it through the Gothic door, scarcely high enough to pass under without stooping, the first object on which her eyes fell was a crimson morocco sketch-book, closing like a pocket-book, nearly filled with sketches.

The last two sketches were—first, an arbour, in which a lady and gentleman are seated; the lady is arranging roses from a basket before her, while her companion reads to her. The last sketch is the empty arbour; the book lies open upside-down on the table, the roses are fallen on the ground. In the pocket was a photo of a lady and gentleman together, the latter in officer's uniform.

" What a contrast to these grim ruins, with all their

legendary memories, is this elegant scrap of modern art!" exclaimed May. "I am sure there is some sad history associated with this little book. Perhaps I may find the owner."

"Warum nicht?" replied the Baronin. "The woman in the Bible found her piece of silver, the shepherd his lost sheep, Saul found his father's asses, Jochebed found her baby, Joseph found his brethren, and poor old Jacob found his long-lost Joseph, and the loser of this sketch-book may be as fortunate."

A few days after this event the Baronin gave a *Kaffee* to à large Gesellschaft, in the park of Schloss Stolzstein. The company sat grouped here and there under the clumps of old beeches and oaks, the deer cast their shadows in the clear lake, graced with swans, and somewhere in the background the music of a military Capelle floated softly on the air.

Mary Rosenmore amused herself with a study of the varied characters present, and with German manners, which were new to her.

A maiden lady, the Baronin von Schattenthal, who was staying at the castle with her young orphan niece, interested her with her quaint humour and sound common sense.

Little Amalia came out with her attendant to her aunt. She was a lovely child, with long auburn curls, and a dash of the French character, for her mother was a Pole.

Finding that her aunt paid no attention to her

toilette nor her curls, Amalia finally whispered, "See, Tante, Gretchen has curled my hair."

"I see, my dear," said the Baronin; "but it will do you no harm if your hair does curl, if you are a good little girl."

Amalia's crestfallen, puzzled look as she walked away were amusing enough.

Soon after she came back with a very knotty question.

"Tante, could all our family ride on an elephant at once? Gretchen says they *could*."

"Yes, child, several small families could ride on an elephant at once."

But May was not left long at leisure to amuse herself with the pretty child.

Her hostess brought and introduced to her Baron von Stammnitz, fresh from the Heidelberg University. She soon found, however, that he was possessed of much finer cultivated hair and moustache than mind. He had dipped a little into the natural sciences, and learned a smattering of some of the absurdities of German Pantheism, and held himself competent to solve the mysteries of creation, and moral relations, of the universe and of mind, much better than the old-fashioned Moses and the Prophets, or St. Paul.

It is this false moral training of the students of Germany that will prove one of her greatest dangers in the future.

Baron von Stammnitz had studied English, and

3

began at once to edify May by airing it.   She expressed her admiration of the Harz, its history and legends.

He replied, " Yes, the Harz is highly interesting, but chiefly so through its old leg-ends."

But let us not be too hard on the Baron in this respect, for the English often make as ludicrous errors in German.   The writer heard a young lady in Cologne order Himmelfleisch, meaning Hammelfleisch.   She intended to ask for mutton, but in reality ordered heaven's meat.   And the waiter, with his solemn, impenetrable face, replied, " I regret we have not that dish."

A gentleman in Leipzig ordered Kinderbraten and Pantoffel—child roast and slippers! He wanted Rinderbraten and Kartoffel—roast beef and potatoes!

People who drop their H's in English do the same in German.   An English girl driving away from Ballenstedt, cried out, " Farewell, Arz ! "

At the hotel by the Radau waterfall an old man ordered the Kellner* to bring beer, and called after him, " Aber ell !"   Hell he meant—clear or white in contrast to brown beer.

He had been parading about and ordering the Kellner as if he owned the whole place, which made his missing H all the more amusing.

But to return to the Baron.   May spoke of the towered village church nestling so confidingly in the rich foliage, and regretted she had not yet seen the interior, but hoped to the following Sunday.

* *Kellner*—Garçon, waiter.

" Pray, Miss Rosenmore, you do not keep up that absurd idea of going to church ? I have not been in a church for five years. While they insist on preaching the old fables that nobody believes any more, I shall not go. I can attend to my religion much better in my own room, or in the woods, where the trees form nobler Gothic arches than any cathedral, from Köln and Halberstadt down. Even meine Mutter told me not to trouble myself about the Bible, for there was no truth in it."

" Woe to any mother who could give such advice !" cried May, in great excitement. She spoke of some of the strongest proofs of the Divine origin of the Bible, and asked the Baron if he could explain why it was that Christian nations were the most elevated, those without the light of revelation being the degraded ones.

" Oh !" said he, " such a view has something beautiful in it ; but it is only a delusion, a transition period in the history and development of mind, I might say, the Raupenkleid — chrysalis — of education, out of which the splendid and brilliant butterfly of free thought breaks forth, and Science unfolds her golden wings, and in her commanding presence, the old orthodox Bible-faith can never again lift its head.

" There is an endless primeval matter, I may say the Urkraft—first cause—of all things, which is scattered in countless atoms in eternal space.

" From this primeval matter, during the course of millions on millions of ages, slowly and gradually unfolded beings, from the most insignificant to the highest. From a scrap of mud, through the effect of light and heat, perhaps by contact with some other body, a frog was produced. Nearest related to the frog stands the Labyrinthodonten, whose hand-like foot-tracks have been found in the sandstone, and which is decidedly the transition between these animals and the higher species of the ape; and from the ape, during impossible-to-comprehend ages, man has sprung, at first rough and animal, as we see to-day in savage races, from step to step unfolding and rising, till we have the Mensch of our present civilization and re-finement."

All this was said with a foppish, self-satisfied air, as if he were the personification of wisdom. May looked at him in amazement, wondering at his shallowness.

At length she said, " Concerning origin and ancestors I will not now dispute. If you deny the Bible, we have no common ground of argument; and if your argument be true, we have after this life—nothing. Let proud Science beware lest she scorch her 'golden wings' in the avenging fire of Divine wrath.

" If you are content with the doctrine of man's descent from an ape, originally, according to your own argument, from a frog! I deny its truth, and claim mine from an eternal, omnipotent and holy Creator, and personal Father, not simply an eviges Sein—eternal state of being—but something infinitely and incomprehensibly more exalted.

Here the conversation was interrupted by the approach of the Baronin, accompanied by a tall noble-looking lady attired in black.

May started, for it was the lady in the photo of the lost sketch-book. Her friend introduced the stranger as the Countess von Omnesky, a lady of Russian birth, but who had been partly educated in England, her father having long filled an official position there under the Russian Government.

The Countess was still young, only five-and-twenty, of a pale, melancholy, but highly intelligent countenance, and her sapphire blue eyes had a mournful, faraway look in them, that touched one deeply.

Their conversation turned on the beauties of Harz scenery, and its romantic ruins, and the Countess remarked she had only the other day visited the Regenstein, and during the day had lost an object, to her of great value—a sketch-book, filled by her late husband, with the exception of the last sketch, which she had herself sketched after his death.

May drew forth the sketch-book, which she had purposely carried in her pocket, and handed it to her, remarking she had recognized her from the photo at the first glance, and explained how it had come into her possession.

The Countess turned to the sketch in the arbour, remarking, " We were sitting thus, when Karl was summoned to join his regiment at the breaking out of the last war between France and Germany. We had only been married three weeks when France declared war, and my joy was broken for ever. If you will not be wearied, I will tell you the history."

May assured her of her deep interest and sympathy, and they seated themselves under a magnificent oak near the lake.

"My sister Olga and I were married on the same day to two brothers, German officers, just three weeks before the commencement of the war. We were in Switzerland at the time of the mobilization of the German army, and hastening to obey the call, we repaired to Berlin, where we took leave of one another, never again all to meet in this world.

"Olga and I remained a short time in Berlin, but after the reports of the battle *bei* Wörth we grew too excited to stay so far from the scene of action, and accordingly went to Baden, taking only our maid with us, and not wishing to go to an hotel, we took apartments in a private *pension* kept by a family from Edinburgh, two old maids and their brother, Mac Stab by name; and though I have travelled over nearly all Europe their equal I have never met, and have reason to believe Scotland or Germany could produce few such creatures.

"You may imagine the difficulties of travelling in time of war, with soldiers being transported to active service, and the sick and wounded to hospitals; and we lost our luggage, consisting only of two trunks.

"We explained to the elder Miss Mac Stab, who

wore a couple of pig-tail curls each side of her face, that our trunks were lost, but we hoped would be found in a day or two.

"The second day passed, but our missing trunks did not appear, in fact never did; and the third morning, as poor Olga was descending the stairs for breakfast, Miss Mac Stab attacked her, crying out: 'See the painted Jezebel! with her curls and diamond rings! The impostor seeks to deceive honest folk with her pretended wedding-ring and tales of lost luggage!'

"Olga, in perfect terror, pale as marble, came rushing to meet me. She could not speak, and did not need to, for I had heard what had passed. I took Olga by the arm, and walked firmly to the breakfast-room. Miss Mac Stab was arranging our breakfast-table as we entered. I inquired if any letters were come.

"Miss Mac Stab glowered at us with an awful face, and replied savagely, in coarse tones, 'Yes! here is a letter; but you wrote and sent it to the post yourselves; nobody would write to the likes of you. Such grand pretensions, with your crests! You'll not get no more letters here; I'll intercept them, and expose your falsehoods.'

"We hastened to our rooms, and sent Paulina to call a carriage. I knew there was an English clergyman in the place—the Rev. William Samper—and we thought it better to acquaint him with our embarrassment, as we were alone, and ask his advice.

"Olga went, taking Paulina with her, and I remained alone. There were two or three strangers staying in the house who had also gone out; hence there was no one but the family at home.

" The day before, on going out for a drive, we had locked our door, and the Mac Stabs denied our right to lock any door, or even to keep any door-key. No sooner had Olga gone, than Miss Mac Stab, accompanied by her brother and sister, came upstairs and entered my room without knocking. Mr. Mac Stab demanded the keys. I told him I should not deliver up the keys till I had done with the apartments, and expressed my surprise at the insolence in thus entering my room unbidden, and the cowardice of such conduct when no one was there to see or hear. Miss Mac Stab, with one sweep of her hand, brushed all my writing materials on the floor, and her no less amiable brother seated himself, saying he should wait till he had the keys. 'You will wait then,' I said, 'until my sister and maid return.'

" 'My maid!' cried Miss Mac Stab. Just then a loud ring hurried them all away.

" I locked my door till Olga returned. She had seen Mr. Samper, and shown our letters, and he would be with us in a few moments. He came and insisted on our going with him, perfect strangers though we were, at once to his house, assuring us Mrs. Samper was expecting us, breakfast was being made ready, and our rooms awaited us.

" The very atmosphere of their house was peace,

and Mrs. Samper was like a mother to us, and the noble Christian pair have the warmest place in my memory and heart. The following day Mr. Samper received a letter from the Mac Stabs, claiming damages for a broken Sèvres vase and an injured piano, amounting to four pounds—all, of course, absolutely false. Mr. Samper wrote, declining any further correspondence, and informed them the post and the law were open.

"Karl and Franz, on hearing our story, sent them a solicitor's letter, demanding an explanation of their infamous conduct to two defenceless ladies. The reply to this letter was absolute silence, and the sudden disappearance of the Mac Stabs from the town. We found they had treated many badly, and had sought in various instances, by driving people to leave before the expiration of the time already paid for, or by involving them in law proceedings, to gain money.

"We stayed a few days with the good minister, but in a state of feverish excitement, watching the descriptions of succeeding battles, and reading the lists of wounded, dead, and missing, with a horrible fascination.

"At last we could bear the uncertainty no longer, and assuming the dresses of nuns, we joined several actual nuns and a couple of surgeons who were going to France to follow the second army, in which Franz and Karl served, to nurse the wounded, seeking them out on the battle-field, which was very necessary, for there were not nurses and surgeons sufficient for the need, and many died for the lack of nursing in time.

"At length came the terrible battle of Mars la Tour —St. Hilaire, or Vionville—in the burning heat of August—the 16th it was—and Major Franz Omnesky was among the missing. Olga set off alone in her wild grief, to search on the battle-field, knowing we would not let her go; and when we first missed her, we had no idea how long she had been gone.

"Oh! how shall I attempt to depict that dreadful night-scene among the dead and dying on the field of Mars la Tour? The pale, ghastly faces looking up to God's pure, blue heavens so *fearfully calm* above all this human woe and anguish!

"Among the heaps of the slain, stumbling over horse and rider, we searched till night grew pale before the dawn, and then we found what we sought —and dreaded to find—Franz dead, and Olga lying with her head on his breast, in a deathly swoon, her garments wet with dew, and her long, beautiful hair falling over her dead husband's face.

"Olga never rallied; the grief, exposure, and fatigue were too much for her delicate frame and passionate love for Franz. We laid them both in one grave, on a knoll, under a clump of limes—the two brave hearts, so true and noble.

"Then came the 18th of August, that most murderous of all the engagements of the war, the battle of Gravelotte, in which the Kaiser commanded in person, with a brilliant staff, Prinz Friedrich Karl, Steinmetz, Moltke, Roon, Bismarck being on it.

"Colonel Karl Omnesky was among the wounded, and I hastened on to nurse him, as I hoped, to renewed life and vigour, but the moment I saw him all hope died for ever. Death was written on his noble brow, but his great, deep violet eyes looked bravely and tenderly as ever into mine. Oh those precious days! Golden is their memory, though so unspeakably sad.

"He was ready to go, awaiting eagerly the change to the better land, but full of tender sympathy and sorrow for me and his unborn child.

"He never was weary of hearing that wonderful prayer of our Saviour, the seventeenth of St. John, and the fifteenth of the First Epistle of the Corinthians.

"Often, accompanied by the harp he so loved, I sang his favourite lines, my heart frantic with grief, but outwardly calm, for God lent me strength.

> " ' Bleibe bei mir vom Morgen bis Abend,
> Denn ohne Dich kann ich nicht leben.
> Bleibe bei mir denn die Nacht ist dunkel,
> Und ohne Dich darf ich nicht sterben.'

> " ' Abide with me from morn till eve,
> For without Thee I cannot live.
> Abide with me when night is nigh,
> For without Thee I cannot die.'

"The noble-hearted Kaiser honoured my dying husband, before the second army moved on, with a visit, and the tear his Majesty brushed away did honour to the Sovereign so deservedly beloved.

"In peace my poor Karl died, and I closed the loving eyes—and my heart died.

"I buried him beside Olga and Franz, and am building a chapel over them.

"Five months after Karl's death my golden-haired Tatjana was born. For her sake I strive to reconcile myself to life.

"But, alas! my wealth and joy are—*a grave!*

"Sitting the other day in the enchanting valley of the graceful Ilse, leaping proudly and gaily in a thousand tiny waterfalls over the moss-grown stones, as if conscious of her royal origin, I wrote the following lines which express faintly my feelings, and which I beg you to keep as a souvenir of our first meeting:

ALONE.

" The sun has set, the evening brightness fades,
  The gloom increases in the forest glades ;
  And a deep sadness all my soul pervades :
                I am alone.

" A wild bird here and there still sings to cheer
  His mate that nestles in the thicket near ;
  But ah ! no voice of love falls on *my* ear :
                I am alone.

" The gentle air plays with the rustling leaves,
  Sweet with the fragrant odours it receives ;
  My bosom with no whispered incense heaves :
                I am alone.

" A distant horn the evening silence breaks,
  The mountain in soft echoes answer makes ;
  No heart responsive to *my* voice awakes :
                I am alone.

"O'er rocky heights the Ilse, wild and free,
Hastes like an eager lover to the sea ;
But whither shall *I* turn for love?   Ah me !
        I am alone.

"Still dreaming dreams I can to none impart,
I live with Nature and my own sad heart ;
Whatever comes of joy or suffering's smart,
        I bear alone."

The following is the German translation :—

Des Abends ros'ger Glanz erbleicht, das Land
Wird dunkel, dunkel wird's am Waldesrand ;
In mir auch nachtet's, einsam ist die Hand :
        Ich bin allein.

Ein Vogel heir und dort dem Weibchen singt,
Das nestlos nahe lauscht, wie's zu ihm klingt ;
Zu meinem Ohr kein Ruf der Liebe dringt :
        Ich bin allein.

Die Blätter lispeln, sie umkost die Luft
Mit sanftem Spiel, einathmend ihren Duft ;
Wer flüstert Balsam mir in's Herz hinein ?
        Ich bien allein.

Ein fernes Horn ertönt mit sanftem Schall,
Der Berg antwortet ihm im Wiederhall ;
Auf meinen Laut erwacht kein Herz im All :
        Ich bin allein.

Es stürzt die Ilse sich vom Felsbett her
In hast'gem Liebeslauf hinab zum Meer ;
Doch ich? wohin? die Welt ist liebeleer ;
        Ich bin allein.

Noch träum' ich Träume, doch sie theilt kein Herz,
Allein mit der Natur und meinem Schmerz,
—Kommt Freude mir, bricht Leid herein :
        Ich trag's allein.

The Flower of the Lauenburg.

BROKEN walls of the grey, long-past centuries, on the wooded mountains, a dilapidated tower, moats overgrown with wild thorns, a few dark and gloomy vaults, and half-fallen windows and arches— those are the small remains of the most magnificent of the former castles of the Harz mountains, the ruins of the ancient seat of the Counts-palatine, the Lauenburg.

In former days the spot lay much more desolate than now; the old ways and the delicious wood-paths had not been opened up.

Heaps of rubbish and shapeless ruins lay scattered everywhere; scarcely could the wanderer break his way through the creepers of the common virgin's bower, and the prickles of the buckthorn over the moss-grown walls, to the broken tower.

But the young people of Dorf Steckelnberg, at the foot of the lower adjacent mountains, on which lie the ruins of Schloss Steckelnberg, found their way easier; it was just the wild and savage character of the place that attracted them, and it was very seldom that a troop of merry boys did not choose the lonely ruins as the scene of their games, and even timorous maidens ventured to approach the haunted walls in their search after berries and wild-flowers.

Once, more than a hundred years ago, on St. John's

Day, a number of children from Steckelnberg were scattered in the thickets around the ruins gathering flowers and making wreaths and garlands, when suddenly one of the boys uttered a cry of astonishment.

The others ran to him, and lo! there stood on the edge of the tower walls, then rising only the height of a man from the *débris* a wonderful flower, the like of which the children had never seen before.

It looked so strange, and still seemed to gaze so mildly and confidentially in the eyes of the children, that they all at once fancied something supernatural in the flower.

They had often heard their parents and grand-parents relate how once, in the greyest times, a maiden had been carried off by the Ritter of the Lauenburg, and in the hour of her greatest danger had been rescued from his power by transformation into a flower, which bloomed every year a single day, and the maiden came and wandered a single night through the ruins.

" Might this be the flower ? " they asked.

At last one of the boys began climbing up the tower walls to pluck it, when he heard a soft voice murmur so clearly that all heard it, " Do not pluck me."

The boy started back in affright ; but, vexed at his fear, feeling sure a flower could not speak, he began again to mount the tower ; but the same voice came from the flower, " Do not pluck me," and the children cried, " Give it up and come down ! "

This excited him still more, and stretching out his hand to pick the flower, a hideous serpent raised its head hissing from under the leaves, when the boy fell back in deadly terror among thorns and fallen stones, and was carried home with broken limbs.

Again, on a St. John's Day, the children of Steckeln- berg played among the ruins of the Lauenburg, when they saw again the wonderful flower, and heard the same soft voice, " Do not pluck me." In affright they fled down the mountain.

But a quiet little girl had remained behind, for it seemed to her the flower did not say, " Do not pluck me," but, " Pluck me." Hence she stood thoughtfully gazing in the flower's clear eye, when again she heard in soft tones, " Pluck me ! pluck me ! "

The maiden came nearer, the flower's glance grew more loving, but under her leaves she saw the serpent- head, which rose hissing and coiling.

Then she drew back her hand, and dared not touch the flower, and as she fled she heard still the voice, " Only pluck me ! "   .

The next day she went back, determined to obey the voice, and pick the flower, but it and the serpent had vanished.

Years fled. The little girl had grown to woman- hood and became the *Braut* of an honest but poor youth.

Then she recalled the wonder-flower and entreating voice, and thought to herself she had missed her good fortune through her disobedience.

This she related to her lover one day as they wandered through the wood around the ruins.

And he strove to comfort her, and thought they were enough in each other, and would be able to support themselves without aid from the world of enchantment; but in his mind he thought she might have gathered the flower, for tales were still told of great treasures guarded by the maid of the Lauenburg, and he had himself already seen much of the wonder-world, and the influence of higher powers over human destiny.

Was he not a Sunday child? *

He was present as the owner of the estate Winatahusen in Thale, had removed the wonder-stone, on which the good fortune of the estate hangs, and had seen how sixteen horses and hundreds of men had only with difficulty moved it; while the heavens had grown dark, and the storm threatened to destroy the buildings, and only misfortune followed misfortune, till the stone was restored to the ancient convent estate.

He had also learned the power of enchantment possessed by the dwellers of the caves in the Bodethal.

* In the Harz it is said all children born on Sunday are always fortunate.

4

A dwarf of one cave had often brought him a bundle of healing herbs for his sick mother, and he knew that he always laid healing plants ready for those who had entreated his help.

But the angry cobold, who in the form of a green bottle-fly dwelt in another cave, had once nearly thrown him headlong from the rocks as he gathered plants, and he only saved himself by making the sign of the cross three times.

He had also seen the blue flame in the garden of the Kloster estate in Thale, which marked the spot where treasures were hidden.

While indulging in these reminiscences a low exclamation from his companion aroused him from his reverie.

She grasped him by the arm, and pointed to the ruins. There, above the tower, rose amid the slender grass, in wonderful beauty, white as a lily and as graceful, the Flower of the Lauenburg, which had just been the subject of their conversation and their dreams.

She seemed to bend her white corolla in greeting, and like a low melody to call down to them, " Pluck me! pluck me!"

The lovers gazed a moment, surprised, at each other ; and, as if the glance had filled him with enthusiasm, the youth then hastened forward, and raised his arm to gather the flower,

At this moment the serpent-head raised itself,

terrible to behold; the scales of the coiled body seemed to bristle, and resemble a coat of mail; the vicious eyes burned in rage, and the sharp tongue pointed at them like a poisoned arrow.

Terrified at the sight, he lost his courage, forgot to cross himself, and, seizing the hand of the maiden, turned to flee.

But she held him back; she stood lost in thought a moment; then pressing his hand warmly and glancing toward heaven, she approached fearlessly the tower, and stretched forth her hand firmly to pluck the flower.

And see! the serpent, though hissing more furiously, drew slowly back its head, and as she plucked the flower fled, and at the same moment the whole scene changed.

Where the flower grew, now stood, sweetly smiling, in swan-white garments, a graceful maiden, who looked kindly on the lovers, and, pointing to a vault at the base of the tower, in which glittered gold and silver vessels of all sorts, stooped and handed one piece after another to the astonished lovers, who took the costly gifts as in a dream.

When they had all they could carry, she waved the hand in farewell, as bidding them to depart, and vanished.

The White Stag.

LONG centuries ago a peculiar appearance attracted the attention of the inhabitants of Dorf Treseburg.

Every morning stood, high on the summit of the Hagedornberg, which rises perpendicular to the banks of the Bode, a White Stag, and gazed fixedly below into the valley.

He stood hours at a time, and had done so over a hundred years, without any variation or the faintest sign of age. Wonderful as this was, it was still more remarkable that no one had ever been able to come near him, although various sportsmen had attempted it, not even when they waited in the early morning on the spot where he was wont to appear.

They waited in vain, and yet at the same time the villagers below had seen him as usual.

So it had come that for a whole generation no one had sought to come near the White Stag. Hence every one shook the head doubtfully when one day an herb-gatherer of the village, named Weidemann, declared that he had not only been near the stag, but that the animal had come close to him, leaned against him, eaten of the plants he carried, and finally had followed him part way down the declivity of the mountain.

The herb-gatherer, however, was known to be a man of veracity, and they soon became convinced of the truth of his statement; for no sooner had he climbed the Hagedorn than the White Stag ran to him, and walked trustfully by his side, ate from his hand, and followed his steps.

This excited all the more surprise inasmuch as the stag avoided everybody else. Weidemann was surprised himself at this confidence, which grew every day; and it seemed to him, when the stag gazed at him with its clear eyes so winningly, as if it would speak, and only language failed.

At last, he said one day to his wife, "There is something the matter with the White Stag, and he longs to tell. If I only could know what it is!"

"That is not so difficult," replied his wife. "Just ask old Fischersche, who will be able to tell thee."

Fischersche was, according to some, a wise, good old woman, according to others a witch, who lived in a hut a little out of the village, never leaving it, alone and without friends, avoiding men and shunned by them in return—but only till they got into some trouble; when illness or some accident had befallen them, then they sought out old Fischersche, related their trouble, and found ever help and counsel, or herbs and healing draughts, before which every sickness fled.

To her the herb-gatherer applied, told her what had happened, and begged for an explanation of the matter.

Fischersche bent her ice-grey head and remained a

while sunk in thought. At length she said : "It is a wonderful history of the White Stag ; my aged grandmother told it me over a hundred years ago, but I cannot now remember it perfectly ! I only know that it is an enchanted young noble, the son of an Earl, but how it all hangs together has escaped me. But we will soon learn. I will ask my ravens."

So saying, she opened the windows of the hut, one towards the north, the other to the south, and murmured a few unintelligible words, and uttered one piercing whistle.

Soon the beating of heavy wings was heard, and a hoarse croaking, and a pair of huge primeval ravens flew down, and sat, one on the north, one on the south window, and cried :

> "Kra ! kra ! kra—h !
> Wir sind da !"

And Fischersche addressed them in a loud voice : " Ye good ravens, ye are as old as the Harz and the primeval forests, and ye know all things ; hence ye shall tell me the history of the White Stag."

Then one raven flapped his wings, nodded with his head, opened his bill and cried :

> " Kra ! kra ! kra—h !
> Ich weiss wie es geschah !"

"The son of an Earl had fallen in love with the daughter of the Ritter who dwelt ages ago in Schloss Treseburg, and came every day and stood on the summit of the Hagedorn, and gazed across to the Treseburg, to see if he could catch a glimpse of the maiden, or a greeting from her.

"It happened once that he met there a noble white stag, and being a passionate lover of the chase, he threw his spear, killing the animal on the spot.

"Just as he was about to detatch the splendid antlers, to hang up in his castle—for a pair of antlers was his coat of arms—the Waldfrau, the powerful queen of the forest and all game, suddenly broke forth from the underbrush with indignation and wrath, for the dead stag had been her favourite, and cursed the youth in words of fury :

"'Thou bloodthirsty man, thou shalt henceforth no more hunt, but be hunted ; thou shalt be thyself a stag in the place of the one thou hast killed and thou shalt wander in these preserves centuries long.'

"And at these words the Earl's son was transformed into that of the stag, and that is the White Stag of the Hagedorn."

The raven nodded three times with his head in confirmation of his tale, and remained silent.

And Fischersche asked further : "Say on, raven who knowest all things, if and how the enchantment may be broken."

Immediately the other raven rose, flapped his wings and cried :

"Kra! kra! kra—h!
Ja! ja! ja!"

"It was a deed of blood! Blood can break the enchantment. If a hunter who has never shed blood gives him blood that belongs neither to man nor beast, and he both drinks and eats it at the same time, the enchantment of the White Stag is broken."

Fischersche would enquire further, but the ravens both remained silent, shook their heads, spread their rustling wings, and flew forth, one up, the other down the roaring Bode, to their Hort* in the steep rocks of the Bodethal, which still bear the name of the Rabenstein.†

When the ravens had disappeared, Fischersche sank in deep thought, and seemed to forget the presence of Weidemann.

"That is a dark saying," she at length said, breaking the silence, and muttered thoughtfully to herself. "Just wait, just wait, I begin to see through the thing. How was it then? Who can break the enchantment?"

"A hunter who has never shed blood," replied Weideman.

"And where may we find such an one?"

"Probably nowhere."

Fischersche looked at him oddly, while a smile flitted over her wrinkled face

"Tell me, then, hast thou ever shed blood?"

The man started at the question.

* Safe retreat in the rocks; usually applied to the eagle.
† Ravens' cliffs.

"God forbid!" cried he hastily. "How canst thou imagine anything so dreadful of me?"

"Well, well, I did not mean it so badly. I know now where I am, and listen well. Thou thyself canst break the enchantment. Thou art called Weidemann,* because thy ancestor was ranger to the knights of the Treseburg; and dost thou not say thou hast never shed blood? So a Weidemann is found, and it is clear why the White Stag has approached thee: he sees in thee his deliverer."

The good Weidemann was speechless with astonishment, but doubted not the truth of Fischersche's words.

"But the blood," he said meditatively—"the blood that I must give him both to eat and drink; the blood that shall neither be of man nor beast—whence shall it come?"

"That is thy affair," said Fischersche, dryly. "That belongs to thy department; for if the blood must not belong to the animal, perhaps it might be found in the vegetable kingdom. Reflect upon it thyself."

And Weidemann leaned his head on his hand in deep thought.

Suddenly his face grew bright, he sprang up and almost fell on the neck of old Fischersche.

"I have it! I have it!" he exclaimed joyfully. "That is the Hypericon, or St. John's Wort. It drops blood

---

* *Weidemann,* or *Waidemann,* signifies sportsman—hunter—ranger.

on St. John's Eve and St. John's Day, and to-morrow will be St. John's Day, and the flower grows abundantly by my garden fence."

Accordingly the next morning he cut a bunch of the St. John's Wort, in which at this time all wonder-power lies, and carried it to the White Stag on the Hagedorn. The stag sprang impetuously forward to meet him, and hardly had he eaten the plants, when the stag took the form of a stately youth, in knightly gold-embroidered doublet, streaming plume in his barret, and baldrick worked in gold and antlers. With beaming countenance and sparkling eyes he embraced the astonished Weidemann, and cried: "Have thanks, thou honest man; thou hast released me, and shalt not go unrewarded. My father, when I return home, will bestow a rich reward on the deliverer of his son. But tell me. I see there only ruins where once a strong castle raised its towers. Who has destroyed it, and where is the radiant daughter of the Treseburg?"

"Ah, Herr!" replied the herb-gatherer sadly, "so long as I can remember, and my parents and grand-parents, no castle has stood there, and neither knight nor maiden has dwelt in its broken walls. Dost thou, then, not know that long centuries have passed since thy enchantment began?"

"Centuries?" cried the young noble in horror.

"Yes, centuries!" exclaimed a scorn-laughing voice, and the Waldfrau stood before them: "that is thy punishment for thy criminal deed. Now go and seek thy lordly family and thy beloved; thou wilt find them mouldering in the vault of the dead.

"Thou mayest find rest, now thy enchantment is broken. But thy punishment is not yet at an end. Every seven years, on this day, thou shalt take the form of my slain White Stag for a single day, and appear on this spot."

With these words the Waldfrau vanished.

The youth shuddered, and said, deeply sighing: "Is it so? Is my age so far in the past? Then truly I have nothing more to find in life. Neither can I find treasures at home to reward thee, honest man. Thou must be content with my baldrick, all that I can give thee, with God's blessing."

And giving him the baldrick, he walked away and was seen no more.

And sometimes still, on St. John's Day, the White Stag is seen on the Hagedorn, gazing with fixed eyes into the peaceful vale.

The Fisherman of Treseburg.

FROM the windings of the Bode, a huge greenstone rock rises steep and rugged, partially overgrown with the *Planta genista*, or wild broom, and creeping plants, nearly its entire base being washed by the waves of the clear mountain stream.

On its summit, half hidden by moss and wild thorns

are grey ruins of a castle, of which no trace of its history is left to us save its name—the Treseburg.

At the foot of this massive rock, on the opposite bank of the Bode, stood, nearly two hundred years ago, a small cottage, in which dwelt a poor but good fisherman, who earned but a scanty subsistence from the fruits of his toil.

At that time thousands of strangers did not, as now, visit the sublime rocky valley, to enjoy its wild and savage grandeur, and its trout and merlins, and the poor man, though naturally of a contented mind, often murmured at his poverty.

Also the romantic situation of his cottage satisfied him no longer, and when he looked across the Bode to the mighty rock, and the ruins on its top, all sorts of foolish and ambitious thoughts crowded his mind.

These reflections were all the more bitter since there was a tradition in the village that he himself was a descendant of the ancient Ritter who once ruled in the Treseburg.

And in fancy he pictured the old Schloss in its former state, throned on the proud rock, with giant round tower, and arched entrance gates, and Gothic windows, the battlements covered with soldiers in steel harness, with sword and lance.

Thus he frequently sat hours at a time by his nets, lost in dreams, ever glancing again across to the wild ruins, and wishing the long-vanished centuries back again.

Once—it was a St. John's Day—he saw a Grau-männchen* on the other side of the stream, who evidently wished to cross, but did not venture to wade through, since the waters had risen in the late thunderstorm, and there was at that time no bridge.

Graumännchen seemed in great embarrassment; this awakened the pity of the fisherman, and he called across that he would come and carry him over the water.

He waded over and did as he had said.

Graumännchen was much pleased at this kindness, thanked the fisherman in the warmest terms, and said, "Thou art a good, obliging man, and since thou hast fulfilled my wish, I could wish that thou also hadst a wish or two that I might grant."

"Ah!" said the fisherman, "every one has wishes. I have just one, but it cannot be realized."

"Only one?" said Graumännchen. "I would grant thee willingly two or three. But what might be thy wish?"

"My greatest wish," replied the fisherman, "is to be set back five hundred years, in order that, instead of that heap of ruins across there, the Treseburg might raise its proud battlements and tower."

"Well," said Graumännchen, "that can easily happen," and he bade him close his eyes for a minute. He did so, and on opening them again gazed around him in wonder, for there opposite on the dark rock

*Graumännchen—Little grey man; a dwarf wood fairy.

stood the Treseburg, that he had so often seen in ruins. Really and truly there it stood, with white walls, colossal round tower at the entrance, battlements shimmering in the sunlight, and squires glittering in steel, with sword and lance.

The fisherman almost devoured the singular picture with his eyes, and in his admiration could not turn away his gaze, till Graumännchen put an end to his puzzlement with the question, "Thy wish is granted; art thou satisfied?"

The fisherman hesitated, for it seemed to him at the moment as if he might add another wish. At the same time the immediate fulfilment of his wish appeared to have its shady sides, for the soldiers who stood on the walls of the castle grew noisy, and called down to him with abusive and threatening words, and commanded him at once to bring up all the fish and other articles of provision which he had, or his last hour was come.

Some even, as if in joke, bent their cross-bows toward him, and one pointed iron bolt lodged in the trunk of a rotten tree close by him.

Finally the fisherman replied, "Yes, the fulfilment of my wish is delightful, and the Treseburg is a right stately Schloss; but I should like, as my ancestors once ruled there, to be transplanted into the position of my ancestor who lived there five hundred years ago, in exactly the same circumstances."

"Very well," said Graumännchen; "also this wish

can be granted," and bade him again to shut his eyes.

When he opened them he found himself in a spacious hall, its stone walls adorned with armour and arms, and on a massive oak table lay also arms, partly broken, partly covered with fresh blood.

From without, a wild deafening noise penetrated to the hall, mingled with loud shouting, sometimes a piercing cry of pain, and the clashing of arms.

He lay himself, in steel armour, on a bench, but one arm was free from armour, and he felt a burning pain in it, and, to his terror, he observed a gaping wound, as from the blow of a sword, stretching from the shoulder to the elbow, and the warm blood trickled down.

Just then a door opened, and an old squire entered and said, " I left you a moment to prepare an ointment for your wound, in order that you may yourself appear on the walls and defend the Schloss. The danger is great, Herr! Listen! They are storming again already, and our men are so weak from hunger and thirst, they can scarcely stand.

" I have obeyed your command, gestrenger Herr— your Lordship—and, in case of the worst, have buried the treasures in the small vault, three times seven paces from the tower westward, and three times seven paces from the entrance gates to the south. But hark! The gates are burst in! We are lost!"

And the old man hastened away. The transformed

fisherman grew dizzy, and felt extremely uncomfortable.

But he had little time for reflection, for the tumult grew louder and came nearer. The door of the hall was broken in with heavy blows, and with loud shouts a troop of men, dripping with blood, rushed in and threw themselves in rage upon him, crying : " We have thee at last, thou foul knave ! thou who hast robbed and murdered so many. At last the hour of retribution has come."

And the leader cried : " Fasten a rope to the arch of the gates, give him an hour to say his prayers, but in the deepest dungeon, and then hang him for a punishment and a warning."

And strong arms seized him and threw him in the dungeon on damp straw.

There he lay, and could not for some time collect his thoughts ; but when he came to his full senses a deep sorrow seized him to see what he had brought upon himself through his foolish wish. Now he must die as a criminal, separated from wife and children, who would never know what had become of him.

" Ah !" cried he in anguish. " Graumännchen ! Graumännchen ! why hast thou done this ? If thou hast granted me, fool that I was, two wishes, so grant me the third—the only one I have—to return home," and hot tears rolled down his face.

But when he had dried his eyes, and opened them again he drew a long breath, for he lay on the banks of the Bode beside his nets, which had filled with fish; and of Schloss and Ritter was nothing to be seen— only the ruins as ever.

Graumnänchen stood by him, pressed his hand, and said, with a friendly smile: "Willst thou be henceforth contented, or hast thou still another wish?"

"*Nein! Nein!*" cried the fisherman decidedly, "I have not a wish but to remain what I am my life long."

Graumännchen took his departure with a smile, and the fisherman's dreams of castle and knight with him.

For many years he related only to his wife what had happened, but as he grew old he told the history to his sons, that they might learn therefrom the same lesson as himself.

They laughed to themselves, and held the whole story for a dream, save one brother, who found something very remarkable in it, and when he had a leisure hour he climbed the rock where the Treseburg had stood, observed the direction of the walls and the moat, and removed the moss, underbrush, and thorns. At last he seemed to have found what he sought.

One clear moonlight night he mounted with hook and shovel to the ruins: there, where once the tower had stood, he measured three times seven paces to the west from the tower, and the same distance from the gate southward. Then he began to dig, and soon came to a vault.

5

The following day the villagers, who had gone to gather sticks, found a vault broken in, and a half-rotten chest open, but empty, and on the ground around lay scattered gold and silver coins with an unknown stamp.

Legend of Volkmarskeller.

ON the borders of the wood stand the ruins of the ancient Kloster Michaelstein, which we pass, and go up the valley, the brook acting as our guide.

It conducts us first past a number of ponds, which formerly supplied the self-denying monks with carp for their fasts, and now swarm with speckled trout.

Low willows adorn the banks, and bathe their locks in the waves, out of which a thick wood of slender reeds springs forth.

Now the vale narrows, magnificent walls of rock rise, and picturesque waterfalls toss themselves down the stream.

Suddenly the forest grows thin; the vale divides itself into two arms, and in the dale to the right we see, close by the red-roofed forage-house for game, grey rocks and ruins.

We ascend this dale, and stand by the ruins of the old church Michaelstein, the mother of the later Kloster.

Beneath the ruins extends a wide cave, which gave rise to the building of the church.

This cave served centuries ago as the dwelling-place of a hermit named Volkmar, and still bears his name. Others of like mind joined themselves to Volkmar, and thus arose the brotherhood, and the forest church.

One can now scarcely trace the site of the walls; fruit-trees run wild, and lilacs mark the spot where once the Kloster garden lay, and besides, no trace of a human habitation where once good and holy men dwelt in the mountain solitude.

This spot—this hermitage—was once a renowned shrine, and thousands flocked here to seek consolation, for in the cave was a grave where were said to rest the bones of the Virgin Mary.

Let us enter the cave, which has two openings, one to the south-east, the other to the south-west; it is of considerable height and breadth, resembling a subterranean chapel, formed of cross-arches, and provided with niches. Near the west entrance is the far-famed tomb of Mary.

The small forest church could boast the protection of the great of the earth. Papal bulls gave indulgences for forty days to all who prayed at, and brought gifts to, the shrine.

The Empress Matilda, the wife of Henry the Fowler, endowed it with lands, and Kaiser Otto loaded it with favours, so that an enlargement became necessary, and hence an hour's distance down the valley the larger and more magnificent Kloster was built.

From the charter granted by Kaiser Otto, we learn that this cave was not first occupied by Volkmar; but that a hermitess, Liutburga, dwelt in it long before. Romance has brought them together.

Volkmar was a stately knight, and Liutburga the fairest of the maidens of the Harz, and they loved each other. In her heart lived only his image, and their souls were knit together.

But the Kaiser challenged his knights to combat against the Wenden,* who still clung to heathenism, and refused to recognize Christianity, or the authority of the Kaiser.

Every true knight marched to the conflict, and Volkmar girded on his sword, and the scarf that Liutburga had woven for him, and bade farewell to his beloved.

She stood on the battlements of her castle, and saw him ride away, and when she could see him no longer her sighs and tears burst forth.

Before the image of the Virgin she knelt daily, and prayed for his return; but her petitions seemed unheeded, for troops of combatants returned from battle, but nowhere could she see the plumed helmet of Volkmar, and all were silent and sad at her questionings.

An inexpressible sorrow seized her, she clothed herself in mourning garments, grew paler than the flower that droops before the mighty frost, and refused to be comforted. She could no longer dwell among men,

* Pronounced Venden.

who understood not her grief, and sought the solitude of the forest.

One day in her solitary ramble she discovered this rocky cave, and here she resolved to retire, and spend the remainder of her days in contemplation and devotion.

But her sorrow gnawed at her heart, and she sank to the earth like a drooping flower. The death-angel came, and kissed away her tears.

But Volkmar was not fallen in battle, but had been only severely wounded and taken prisoner by the Wenden, and led away into their deep forests, and it was long before they gave him back his freedom.

He fled on the wings of love to the castle of Liutburga, and hearing of her retirement he penetrated the mountains to seek out the spot. At last he discovered the cave, and his heart was ready to burst with bliss.

He loudly called her name, but no voice answered, only the echo of the mountains. He climbed the mountain, and reached the entrance to the cave. There lay Liutburga in the moss. "She sleeps!" he thought.

Yes, she slept. The cheeks were ashy pale, the eye broken, cold and still the lips; she awoke no more at his call.

The birds of the wood had sung her death-song, and the trees had showered their leaves and blossoms over the still form.

Volkmar returned no more to the world, which had nothing to offer his broken heart.

Where Liutburga had dwelt in her grief was now his home ; the crucifix before which she had knelt was his sanctuary, and henceforth he turned all his thoughts to God, and to the consolation of the sorrowing.

That is the Liutburga of romance. The Liutburga of history * is indeed a highly interesting and noble personality, if less poetic.

Countess Gisela, of the Harzgau, whose seat was Blankenburg Schloss, after the death of her husband, Earl Unwan, built Kloster Wenthusen, and other convents and churches.

Once on a journey she was overtaken by the darkness, and took refuge in a Kloster.

Among the nuns who welcomed her, one, Liutburga, won her affections, and on leaving, Gisela took her home with her.

After Gisela's death, Liutburga, with the consent of Bishop Thiatgrin, of Halberstadt, retired to this cave somewhere between 827 and 840, in which Bernhard, son of Gisela, built her a cell and a chapel.

She was renowned for sanctity and good works, and endowed with a superior mind.

A priest of the cathedral of Halberstadt wrote her biography more than a thousand years ago.

We return to the later Kloster Michaelstein, which is not so rich in poetic legends.

* See *History of Blankenburg*.

Not even a ghostly monk haunts the ruins, nor wanders by moonlight in the venerable cloisters. But on the mountains that surround the dale the two monks, Hans* and Henning, still hold guard.

Once the Abbot, fearing the attack of an enemy, sent the unfortunate brothers out to watch, with the command not to return till the enemy approached.

No enemy came, and the Abbot forgot to recall the monks.

They watched conscientiously till they became stone pillars, and stand still there. The face of one, Hans, is of admirable beauty.

There is a legend that once when the enemy stormed the gates, St. Michael suddenly appeared over the entrance in a flame, with countenance of wrath and drawn sword, at sight of whom every man fled.

Reinhilde of the Königsburg.

THE Königsburg stood on the right bank of the Bode, on a mountain not far from Bodfeld. Originally it belonged to the Saxon Kaisers. The Sausenburg was on the left bank of the Bode, about an hour's walk from Elbingerode. Of the latter nothing is now left save the hewings in the stone masses which formed its foundations. From the battlements of its tower the hunting-castles Bodfeld and Königsburg could be seen.

* Pronounced Hants.

In this romantic neighbourhood, in the thick fir forest, stand the crumbling tower and scraps of broken walls of the Königsburg, overshadowed by the green veil of the wood, moss, ivy, and wild-flowers, and the mystic fascination of a time more than a thousand years ago.

Desolate stand the ruins of the once imperial hunt-ing-seat, the moat so thickly overgrown with the buckthorn that no human foot would willingly at-tempt to tread it.

A light sighing stirs in the foliage like a ghostly breath from the primeval days.

Dost thou remember the time when we listened to the rustling and moaning of the fir-trees, like echoes of the voices of olden times ?   In our dreams we saw the ancient Königsburg in splendour, heard the forest ring with the noise of the hunt, saw the troop of huntsmen ride back to the castle, among them many a knight, earl, and prince, and foremost rode the Kaiser, with his blushing daughter Reinhilde.

How radiant was the royal maiden, her green veil floating on the breeze, her clear eyes gazing fearlessly around her, her sweet face smiling like a bright morning in spring !

The Kaiser bends to her and whispers in her ear.

Why do her blushing cheeks turn pale ?   What has caused the smile to vanish so suddenly from her face, and the tears to rush to her eyes ?

She turns in fear, and looks upon her following

train. Why does a noble, knightly countenance there also turn pale?

The Kaiser glances in surprise at his blushing daughter.

"Dear little Reinhilde, have I grieved thee? Hast thou understood me? Two princes beg the honour of thy hand."

Reinhilde raises her eyes with firmness to his and replies: "Dear father, forgive, but I do not seek for crowns. Thou thyself hast not hidden from me how heavy is the crown. Thou hast often told me that only love makes happy; and I have found a love deep and pure, and could shout for joy; a heart, a knightly heart, is mine. Oh! do not tear this true and noble heart from mine."

The Kaiser frowns, and the anger-vein swells on his brow as he replies: "Dost thou dare to speak thus to me, thou shameless girl? Who is the low knave, the insolent coxcomb, who has dared to raise his eyes to the Kaiser's daughter? My rage shall crush him; ruin on his head who has robbed me of the joy of my old age—the heart of my daughter."

All stand aghast at the Kaiser's wrath, all save one noble knight, who steps fearlessly forth from the circle, with head proudly raised, a youth of manly beauty, the blond locks falling on his shoulders, the blue eyes blazing in just indignation, approaches the Kaiser, and cries, "Herr Kaiser, it was not a 'knave.' At the breach on the bloody field thou hast said, 'Brave

Werner, thou art my bravest hero!' And thou hast chosen me as companion for thy kingly son. Oft hast thou said to me, 'For Werner's faithfulness where shall I find a worthy reward?' Herr Kaiser, now thou hast the reward; take back the word of scorn; listen to the voice of love; make two hearts happy."

Gently Reinhilde clasps the father's hands; but the anger-vein swells higher on the imperial brow.

"Throw the traitor in the deepest dungeon, in chains!" he cries; "and thou, whom I disown as daughter, get out of my sight; let me never see thee again!"

The Kaiser sets spurs to his steed and rides to the Schloss, the attendants bring the unhappy knight to the dungeon, Reinhilde faints and sinks from her steed in the grass, and soon no sound is heard save the sighing in the firs.

With heavy head resting on his arm, the Kaiser sits alone in the great hall of the Königsburg.

Suddenly he starts wildly to his feet; was that a moan that fell upon his ear? No, 'tis only the rattle of the hoarse weathercock. Hark! surely that is a cry of anguish. He listens in agony.

"No, no!" the watcher cries from the tower. He hears the moaning of the tempest, and rain and hailstones beat against the windows.

In heartrending tones the Kaiser cries, "Reinhilde! It was too hard and cruel; a loving word had been better."

Quickly he calls his old servant. " Alter,* bring me my little daughter."

The servant trembles in terror, and tears burst forth.

" What ails thee, Alter ?" cries the Kaiser.

" Herr Kaiser, thou knowest thy little daughter is not here ! Thou hast disowned her."

The Kaiser stares at him in horror, " Reinhilde not here ? Since when ?"

" Herr Kaiser, since yesterday. She has not returned to the Schloss ; her steed came back without its rider. We sent out messengers, but none have found her."

The Kaiser turns pale.

" And thou hast not told me till now ! Reinhilde, Reinhilde not here ? Merciful God ! Reinhilde, my child ! Lost in the forest in storm and tempest ! Up ; ring the alarm ! To horse ! to horse ! Let loose the hounds in the forest ; let the horns resound that my child may know the father calls. Bring me my steed, I will myself ride forth into the storm."

And a thousand torches light up the forest, and the echo of a thousand voices rings far and wide. And the Kaiser's voice combats with the storm as he cries, " Reinhilde ! Reinhilde ! my little daughter !"

At length despair seizes the father's heart, he throws himself to the earth in wild agony, beats his brow and tears his hair, while a troop of attendants stand weeping around him.

* Old man.

With a sudden light in his face, he springs to his feet and exclaims, "Back to the Schloss! There is one who will find Reinhilde, but that one pines in the dungeon. He has loved her like me. I know his love is true; the God of love will be with him; *he* will find my little daughter." And the Kaiser commands, "Let Werner be set free! And when he finds Reinhilde, she herself shall be his reward; let her be his wife, and he my son!"

In the dark mountain cave, on the hard, cold ground, kneels the silver-haired hermit Volkmar, and without before the entrance, by the image of the Virgin, Reinhilde, pale and trembling, is kneeling, in prayer. She vows to become the bride of heaven if the Kaiser does not relent.

The good old man, when she came yesterday telling him all her sorrow, received her lovingly, and gave her a secure refuge in his peaceful retreat. "Stay here, my daughter," he said; "hope and trust in God."

Hark! The horns are heard, and Volkmar rises hastily from his knees and cries, "Quick, in the cave, Reinhilde, that no one see thee; the way leads close by the Virgin's shrine."

The searchers come, and cry, "God greet thee, Volkmar! Hast thou not seen the Kaiser's daughter?"

And Volkmar replies, "I have only seen a bride of heaven, who is resting in the cave."

They ride on, and Volkmar asks the trembling

Reinhilde, "Hast thou heard? They are seeking thee."

"My father has disowned me. I stand alone. Only in the Kloster can I find a home."

And now a single man approaches, stops by the entrance, throws himself on his knees before the shrine of the Virgin, and as Reinhilde hears the voice she trembles and turns pale, for the Kaiser it is who prays.

She exclaims in anguish, "It is my father, but I do not answer, for he has disowned me his child. I stand in the world alone. Only in the Kloster can I find a home."

The Kaiser rides forth with his train, and a knight comes on foot and alone, kneels before the shrine and prays, and at the sound of his voice Reinhilde's eye grows bright.

His prayer ended, his voice rings mightily through the forest as he cries, in love and longing, "Reinhilde! Reinhilde!"

And a silvery voice answers, "Who calls Reinhilde?"

The Kaiser, who is yet near, turns in joyful surprise in the direction of the voice. "Merciful Heaven!" he cries, "hast thou heard our earnest petitions?"

See! From the dark cave issues a light form, and a cry of joy resounds through the whole forest. And in a blissful embrace kneel before the Kaiser Werner and Reinhilde.

The Twelve Knights of the Schöneburg.

ABOUT a Stunde* from Treseburg, up the Bode, lies the picturesque foundry village Attenbrack, the spot where in the old days Schloss Schöneburg looked down from its high, steep mountain seat into the vale below.

On three sides the mountain rises steep from the Bode, being scarcely approachable save from the south side; and in wild confusion lie scattered over the mountain sides shapeless heaps of fallen stones, the sole ruins of the once stately castle; of walls and vaulted chambers no trace remains.

On the south side the height is connected by a narrow tongue of land with the vast forests that cover the high table-lands of the Harz.

Seldom is the spot trodden by the foot of man, except by some benighted traveller, some inquisitive student of history, and the passionate lover of wood and mountain solitude.

More frequently resounds the tread of the hunter in this lonely spot, and of the herdsman, who pastures his cows in the beech forest.

Once a herdsman stood, on St. John's Day, on the narrow path leading to the then not entirely fallen

---

* *Stunde*, speaking of distance in Germany, signifies the distance a man can walk in an hour. It is about a German mile, which is equal to four and seven-tenths of an English mile.

walls, and dreamed of the days of the past, of the Burg and its knights, dames, and maidens, and the treasures that were said to lie concealed under the ruins.

The forest rustled mysteriously, mingled with the dreamy tinkling of the cow-bells.

Suddenly it seemed to him he heard a rumbling noise and loud merry laughter. This was wonderful, but what he saw was still more astounding. For, stealing forward and looking over the broken walls, he saw twelve knights in antique costume, who amused themselves with the game of skittles.

The herdsman was not sure whether he was awake or dreaming. He rubbed his eyes, and looked bewildered around him, but it could be no illusion, for there stood the oaks and beeches, every tree of which he knew, there grazed his herd to the music of their jingling bells, the dogs cowering watchfully near, and from the valley could be heard the rattle of the foundry.

He saw it all clearly, for it was mid-day, and there within the mouldering walls the twelve knights played on, and he heard the rolling and bouncing of the balls.

But he had not much time for observation, for the knights caught sight of him, and beckoned him to approach.

He did so trembling.

They treated him gruffly and severely, and commanded him to set up the fallen pins, and he was obliged to yield.

Perhaps an hour had passed in this employment, when lo! no ball more rolled, and looking up to see the cause of the delay, the knights had vanished!

It was not a dream, for all the pins lay there before him; but knowing that his neighbours in Attenbrack would hold him for a dreamer without proof, he decided to take the pins home with him.

But they were so large and heavy, he could not carry them all, so he took only the king.

All listened incredulously to his tale of the knights and old dress, and feared he was not quite right in his head.

Then he drew forth from his pocket the pin, as proof; but it was so heavy he could not hold it, and it fell to the ground with a clear ring; when, lifting it up, it was found to be pure gold.

No one doubted longer, but all hastened to the ruins to get the other eight pins; but they were all only of wood—of light Taxus wood.

The Gegensteine.

IN the midst of the bright landscape opposite Schloss Ballenstedt rise the two huge boulders called the Gegensteine, which mark the eastern termination of the Devil's Wall.

The taste and passion for the wonderful and mysterious are too strong in the human mind to permit of these majestic rocks being without their *Sage*.

In the time long ago, when all this district was covered with dense forests, swamps and morasses, where now ripen the golden corn, fruits, and every blessing that crowns the husbandman's toil, and wild beasts preyed on the around-lying mountains, evil spirits practised their devices in the Gegensteine.

In the distance one could see during the night, especially at midnight, now fiery balls, now flames of fire rising in the air, and could hear death cries, or the most delightful tones, which the evil spirits employed to decoy unwary mortals to destruction.

Many who ridiculed the idea of danger, paying no heed to friendly warnings forced their way through thorns and thickets to behold the mystery, and returned no more.

They were carried by demons through the air, and one heard their moanings of despair without the power to save them.

Only he who was consecrated to God could approach the Gegensteine unharmed.

One morning a farmer rode before sunrise from Ballenstedt to Quedlinburg, to offer prayers and obtain absolution in the convent church, only just founded by the Kaiserin Matilda—for in Ballenstedt there was neither church nor pater.

Lost in devotional thoughts, hence without fear, he

6

rode quietly along; an irresistible languor seized him and he fell asleep.

The nag, feeling no longer the hand guiding the reins, turned aside to seek for himself a fresh breakfast, stood still, and began to graze.

The farmer awoke. He rubbed his eyes in amazement, for he found himself in an unknown spot, in a dark thicket, without road or path; all round him towered mighty rocks, that almost shut him in. He heard the roaring of water outside, beneath him a raging din, and before him yawned an awful chasm.

The farmer had never heard of such a wild and savage scene so near his place of residence, and fancied he had been transplanted through enchantment to some distant land. Anxiously he gazed around him, convinced himself he was not dreaming, for the sun was shining upon the savage rocks, and his nag grazed unconcerned.

The thought occurred to him he might be in the domains of wicked spirits, and a cold shudder ran over him; but he lacked the courage to turn back, fearing some monster might follow him. He was indeed in a painful position, for it was out of the question that he should remain where he was.

Meanwhile the terrible din and roar had ceased, all grew peaceful, the birds sang joyfully in the sunlight, and all notion of danger vanished from his mind.

He gained confidence as he looked around him to mark the place, resolving next day to bring his wife and children to see it, and convince them that all the tales about the terrors of the Gegensteine were untrue.

"But what may there be in the cave yonder?" he thought.

He would like to know, and now arose a struggle between curiosity and fear.

"I will venture it!" he cried, dismounted, tied his horse to a tree, and went with light steps, as if afraid some one might hear him, over the fallen rocks, and stretched his neck to look into the cave.

"Jesus, Mary, and Joseph!" he cried, clapping his hands together above his head; "what do my eyes see?" And what did they?

In the middle of the pit, or cavern, a large brewer's copper, full of gold pieces, every one as large as the palm of the hand.

Upon it rested a silver tray with a border of fiery carbuncles, and letters and figures in the centre formed of garnets.

Beside the copper lay a new driving whip, and on the other side lay a savage black bull-dog.

The farmer stood with crossed arms for at least ten minutes, gazing at the immense treasures, thinking what was to be done to secure them without falling into the power of the savage guard—the dog.

At last he exclaimed, "I will attempt it. I will not take much, but I must have the whip!"

Encouraged, he walked into the cave, his eye always

fixed on the dog, till at last he reached the copper; the dog did not move; he plunged both hands into the gold coins, filled his pockets, and with two leaps .reached his horse, where he sank down overcome with terror and joy.

Recovered, he emptied his pockets, counted the glittering coins, and dreamed thereby of a happy future.

His horse neighed and pawed the ground impatiently.

" Patience, old nag !" he cried ; " I must have that beautiful whip." And again he descended emboldened into the cave, seized the whip, and turned to go, when his eye fell again upon the tempting gold ; he could not resist the allurement, and plunged both hands twice into the copper.

At the second handful the dog rose and ground his teeth in rage ; but Jacob had lost all fear, and cried, " Growl away ; but one must have all good things three times, and I shall take another handful."

But as he did so the eyes of the dog shot fire, an awful groaning, and noise, a raging storm, thunder, lightning, with cracking of the rocks, broke forth in fury. The earth trembled, the rocks fell upon each other, trees were rent into splinters, torrents burst from the rocks, and the heavens enveloped themselves in night and flames.

The unlucky farmer never knew how he got out of the cave ; only, as he came to himself, he remembered having seen the *Gott-sei-bei-uns** in the midst of a terrible confusion and fire-rain in giant form, surrounded by a thousand imps, rise out of the pit, holding in one claw the copper, with the gold, in the other the tray.

Was he or had he been dreaming? No, *for had he not the whip in his hand?*

But the tremendous weight in his pockets weighed him down. Rejoiced to think of his treasure, he dived into his pockets for the gold—and what did he find?

For every piece of gold a pebble, as large again, and not one piece of gold!

He stared at the stones, crying and trembling with pain and distress.

Still weeping, he mounted his horse, reached home, sank exhausted, laid himself down in his bed, from which he never rose; and in a fortnight he lay in his grave.

Since then the foul fiend has guarded his treasures in the Gegensteine, and in only one way can the enchantment be broken and the treasure won.

When a maiden, born on the ocean, pure as the dawn, comes here alone at the midnight hour of Hallowe'en, kneels and with raised hand calls her own name aloud three times, and then entreats the Most High to break the enchantment, and annihilate the

---

* *Gott-sei-bei-uns*—"God be with us." A name given to the devil; since when he appeared in disguise to deceive people, he is said to have used this hypocritical expression.

monster in the rocks, they shall sink at her prayer, the treasures of gold and gems shall rise to the surface, become the maiden's possession, and the hobgoblin shall vanish for ever.

The Three Crystal Goblets and Three Golden Balls of Schloss Falkenstein.

THE Lady von Falkenstein was once summoned by the *Berggeist** to attend the Queen of the Gnomes in her extremity. He conducted her through long dark subterranean passages to her fairy Majesty; and, after the birth of a son, the Queen presented her with three golden balls and three crystal goblets, with the warning to preserve them well, for the fate of the Asseburgs was closely connected with them.

The three golden balls have been unhappily lost, and only two goblets remain.

Two sons of the family when visiting their widowed mother at Wallhausen, besought her to permit them to drink out of these mysterious goblets, which she imprudently allowed; and as they struck their glasses together with a merry *prosit*, one was shattered.

Deep melancholy seized the youths, and during their drive home the wild horses plunged with the carriage into a deep abyss, where the youths were found broken in pieces.

Since then the two remaining ghostly gifts have

* *Berggeist*—spirit of the mountains.

been sacredly preserved—one, of green-yellow glass, in Hinneburg; the other, of mountain crystal, in Falkenstein.

Tidian's Höhle, or Cave.

BELOW Schloss Falkenstein, in the valley where the gentle Selke winds through her flower-strewn paths, the shepherd of the Graf von Falkenstein grazed his sheep on the dew-gathering meadows.

It was the morning of St. John's Day, and every Harzer knows that St. John's Eve and St. John's Day are rich in miracles in these mountains, and unfold many a mysterious flower.

Not only at this time is the St. John's wort gathered, which is said to bear a red dewdrop at midnight—hence called St. John's blood—and to be a sure remedy against every disease; but also the *Spring-wurzel*, or caper-spurge, which bursts open gates, and even opens the earth and the rocks; the magic wand—*Wünschelruthe*—Aaron's rod—which points out the spot where buried treasures or the precious metals lie hidden; and the *Wunderblume*—marvel of Peru—which opens the eyes of him who is so fortunate as to find this wonder-flower, so that he sees sunken or enchanted castles, and discovers untold riches in gold, diamonds, and rubies.

Tidian found a tiny blue flower, attracted to it by its perfume and its beauty, which must have been one of the miracle-working plants, for no sooner had he stuck it in his hatband than a never-before-seen cave in the side of the mountain opened its splendours to his dazzled eyes.

He entered it, his mind full of tales of buried treasures, filled his pockets with the glittering sand and stones, with the intention of offering them for sale to a jeweller in Aschersleben.

They proved to be more valuable than he had hoped, and the jeweller begged him to sell to no one but himself.

The fame of this gold speedily spread, and it happened that Graf von Falkenstein himself visited the goldsmith, when by chance this gold was spoken of.

"Yes," said the jeweller, "it is indisputable that Tidian's gold is as good again as any other."

"Tidian's gold!" cried the Earl, surprised. "Why do you give it that name?"

"The man from whom I buy it is Tidian."

Instantly it occurred to the Earl that his shepherd Tidian had lately grown rich, and he might be the seller. His avarice awoke; he hastened home, and demanded to know the cause of Tidian's wealth.

True of heart, the shepherd told him everything, showed him the concealed way to the cave, and in company they carried away much of the costly treasure; till at last avarice awaked the fear in the mind of the Earl that Tidian might at some future time reveal the secret to some one else.

This thought left him no peace. At length, to make himself secure of the entire wealth of the cave, he put out Tidian's eyes and shut him up in the castle dungeon.

Then the Earl hurried alone to the cave; he did not know that the flower which Tidian wore in his hat caused the cave to remain open.

The unhappy shepherd tore the flower in pieces, stamped upon and cursed it and the cave, and wished it to close and never again to open until, among the descendants of the Earl, a lame, a dumb, and a blind Falkenstein had ruled.

Immediately the cave shut with a thundering noise, and the greedy Earl wanders there yet, for the enchantment is not yet broken.

The Mägdesprung* and Mägdetrappe.†

IN the valley of the Selke, that fair Undina of the Harz, near Alexisbad, rises the majestic rock Mägdesprung; and opposite, on the other bank of the river, the Mägdetrappe, both of which are so famed in fable.

In the latter rock one sees the impressions of giant feet, and Romance attempts to account for them. She is at least as competent to do so as anybody else.

---

* _Mägdesprung_—maiden's leap.
† _Mägdetrappe_—maiden's footprint.

A giant virgin of the grey primeval times saw from the Mägdesprung her lover on a mountain on the opposite bank.

Her ardent love draws her to him, but she cannot climb the steep rocks, nor swim the Selke, then a torrent.

So she dares—for what will not love dare?—to leap over the wide space that divides the two rocks, leaving the impress of her feet in the rock, since called the Mägdetrappe.

Another *Sage* has a totally different motive.

A maiden of the Huns, a disciple of Diana, roaming fearlessly through the vale, hears from the Mägdesprung a cry of distress. She recognizes the voice that cries for aid, and her eagle eye perceives her friend being dragged away by two mountain robbers.

Her blood boils, and in the anguish of her soul the brave Hun maiden leaps the abyss, falls like an avenging angel upon the villainous mountaineers, with two blows of her spear pierces them both to the heart, and conducts her friend and favourite—for she is said to have been a Hun Queen—home to her parents.

Sage of Schloss Questenberg.*

THE Ritter Knaught had a lovely little daughter, whose chief pleasure was to gather wild-flowers; for this purpose she went often with her nurse into the forest. But one day her nurse lost sight of her, and not being able to find her, hastened in great terror to the castle to give the alarm.

The Ritter summons all his retainers with a horn, and they storm through the forest whole nights and days, but of the lost child no trace.

At last one day, as the father gazes from the battlements of the castle, he sees people approaching bearing the Maien,† hears their shouts of joy, and in their midst beholds his lost Rosamund, decked as Queen of May!

A coaler had met the child wandering through the wood, took her at first for an angel, and in his hut the retainers had found her.

The happy father bestowed gifts lavishly, and instituted an annual *Volksfest*, and called his castle Questenberg.

To this day a popular festival is held here, but whether connected with this tradition is uncertain.

*Questen —wreaths or garlands of flowers.

†Maien—green branches of the birch used to deck the Maypole, and in Thuringia and other parts of Germany the churches at Pentecost.

The youths of Agnesdorf have the right by an ancient statute, of digging up a young oak on the Questenberg ;* the tree must be *carried*, and after it is planted is decorated with wreaths of flowers.

They then go in procession to the parsonage, conduct the pastor to the church, when Divine service is held ; after which all return in procession to the newly-planted oak, and after all have partaken of refreshments they dance around it, and the youths shoot at the target.

Barbarossa and the Kyffhäuser.

O N this mountain that overlooks the Golden Plain, amid the beech and oak woods that clothe it, stand the ruins of a square tower built of red sandstone, broken walls and arches of the ancient gateway, gables, and the remains of the chapel of the fortress, where the first Electors and Emperors of Germany held their court.

Tradition and romance linger with an irresistible fascination around these lonely ruins.

Tradition tells us that Barbarossa never died, but remains enchanted in the heart of the Kyffhäuser.

He sits in an ivory chair by a marble table, his head resting upon his arm, and his long, red beard has overgrown the whole table like moss. He wears the

* The custom of digging up the young oak is now limited to once every fifteen years.

imperial mantle, and the knightly forms of his old courtiers, like spectres, come forth from their rocky chambers and place upon his aged uncovered head the oldest crown of Germany glittering with diamonds. His innocent daughter is the only attendant, or, according to other legends, a dwarf.

The Kaiser's eyes are closed, but at times he seems to awake from his enchanted slumber, and new life seems to animate the stiffened limbs. But he cannot awake, nor rise from his seat, nor leave the enchanted chamber until Germany's enemies are fallen and she is free. He seemed about to throw off the enchanted fetters in the days of Maximilian, again in Luther's time.

At the time of the Rhine Treaty, and when the first Napoleon won the brilliant victories of Ulm, Austerlitz, and Jena, the eyes of the old Redbeard sparkled with anger and grief, and at his cry of rage, lightnings flashed through the dark chambers of the Kyffhäuser, thunders rolled through its rocky caverns, and Barbarossa slumbered again till the great victory of the Allies in the "Battle of the Nations"* awaked him, and at the death of Napoleon on St. Helena he broke the enchantment, and Napoleon sits in his place.

There are many versions of this legend.

One holy day, a miner rambling to the Kyffhäuser, to rest under the trees and indulge in devotional reflections, saw, as he reached the ruined tower, a monk

* *Völkerschlacht*—battle of Leipzig.

with a long grey beard, who addressed him, saying, "Come! I have long expected thee; thou shalt see the enchanted Kasier. Graumännel has brought me the *Springwurzel*,* and I must have a mortal to accompany me; no evil shall befall thee."

The monk leads him to a green spot surrounded with walls, forms with the staff which he carries a circle around him and his companion, takes from his pocket a gold-coloured velvet book, and begins to murmur and read, no word of which the miner understands.

Suddenly there is a terrible clap of thunder. The mountain cracks, the circle on which they stand becomes loose, and sinks slowly into the mountain; the miner, in terror, clings to the cowl of the monk. At last they reach firm ground.

Now they go through a long dark passage to great brass gates. The monk touches them with the *Springwurzel*, and immediately they open. They enter an aisle, lighted by a brilliant lamp, and again stand before a door.

The monk cries, "Hephata!" and the doors open.

They enter a large, brilliantly-lighted, magnificent chapel; the walls are of marble; the altar is of beaten gold, and its eternal lamp bathes all in a wondrous light.

The miner cannot gaze enough at the marvellous sight, crosses and recrosses himself; the monk kneels

*See Tidian's Cave.

at the golden altar and says an *Ave Maria.* Then he rises, commands his companion to remain standing in the middle of the chapel, and approaches the door opposite the one by which they had entered.

At his mighty word this door opens also.

The imperial chamber, or throne-room, is brilliantly lighted; on the glittering golden throne, in imperial robes, sits Barbarossa,* sad and silent.

The monk approaches the enchanted sovereign and bows reverently.

The Kaiser returns the greeting graciously, and the monk lifts with great solemnity some object from the ground, again bows low before the monarch, and retires slowly to the door, seizes the hand of the astonished miner, who has gazed as in a dream at the splendour of the enchanted chamber, leads him to the green circle, which begins at once to rise, and soon reaches the summit of the mountain.

The miner draws a long breath, receives two small metal rods from the monk, who exclaims, " *Gelobt sei Jesus Christ!*" and before the bewildered man can respond, "*In Ewigkeit!*" the mysterious monk has vanished.

* *Barba*, the beard; *Rossa*, red.

The Burgfräulein * of Osterode.

ONE Sunday morning early, a poor linen weaver was walking to Osterode.

Aurora showed her gaily laughing and blushing face above the green mountains, a balsamic freshness floated over the valleys and streams, the peaks of the woody heights swam in the blue ether, and the dew-bathed mountain flowers sparkled in the sun's golden splendour. The songs of the birds rang out of the thickets, and soft chimes rose from the villages summoning to worship and praise—a mild, blissful peace hovered over the entire scene.

It was long before the wanderer noticed these surrounding beauties of the morning, for a heavy sorrow lay at his heart. A beloved wife lay at home ill, six hungry children waited with her anxiously for his return, and he must return with empty hands.

His rich cousin, from whom he had hoped for assistance, had repulsed him with cruel words, and now his future lay dark and hopeless before him.

But as the sun rose higher, as all Nature bloomed and sent forth her frankincense of praise, and the streams murmured of peace, he grew more composed.

"How glorious! how wonderful!" he thought, as he stood still and gazed around him; "and what a mystery it is that only man is so often shut out from

* *Burgfräulein*- castle fairy.

the universal enjoyment of creation. Why should he be crushed to the earth, and provide in sorrow and pain for his bodily sustenance, while the birds sing and the flowers bloom free from care ? Doth He not clothe the lilies, and give the rose and violet their perfume and exquisite hues ? Can the Eternal Father care less for an immortal soul ? No, no, never !"

He began again to move forward, singing that noblest hymn in the German language, which has been so perfectly translated by John Wesley, beginning—

" Befiehl Du Deine Wege." *

When he came to the lines—

" Auf! auf! Gib Deinem Schmerze
Und Sorgen gute Nacht.
Lass fahren, was das Herze
Betrübt und traurig macht !"—

he quickened his pace with a firmer tread and lighter heart.

Perhaps he would have sung on to the end of the hymn, had not a voice, clear as a silver bell, greeted him with "Guten Morgen !"

The singer looked in the direction of the voice, and stood like one transfixed at the sight of the vision before him.

On the banks of the brook which flowed past his

* Commit thou all thy ways.

7

path sat a lovely maiden clad in white, and bathed her marble-white feet in the crystal water.

Before he could recover from his astonishment, the figure rose and approached him, saying in a voice of the most delicious melody—

"Thou sangst just now a beautiful song, that was made for the troubled. May help be as near every one who sings it as to thee; for know, thou art come at a most happy hour. It is only permitted me once a year to be at this spot; and whoever meets me here and deserves it as thou, him I make happy—if wealth can make him happy. Listen, then: when the bells ring midnight, leave thy cottage, and climb the mountain in silence to the ruins of Burg Osterode. Between the sunken walls thou wilt find a flower; pluck it, and instantly all the treasures of the heart of the mountain will be revealed to thine eye, from which thou mayst take as much as thou wilt. Go now thy way, and carry comfort and hope to thy wife. My time is expired."

The slender form, the pale, loving face, transparent as moonlight, the long golden hair, were in a twinkling vanished.

Wonderfully cheered, the weaver hastened home and related his vision to his suffering wife and little children, and they waited with impatience for the appointed hour. At last the leaden-footed hours had passed—it was midnight.

The weaver kissed his wife and hastened forth. It

was a glorious night. The full moon shone, the quail sang her nightly song. The picturesque ruin contrasted wonderfully in its dark grey masses with the cloudless blue of the heavens and the silver moonlight.

A peculiar light shone out of an arched chamber; he followed it, and there sat the pale maiden, adorned with a wreath of white roses in her hair. She raised her jasper-blue eyes, looked kindly on him, and beckoned him to approach and gather the shining flower.

The weaver obeyed and tremblingly plucked the lily.

Hardly had he the flower in his hand when a fearful, rumbling sound arose in the heart of the mountain the ground close to his feet sank crashing into the depths, and a huge cauldron rose in flame, filled to the brim with glittering gold pieces. The maiden bade him take what he would, for he was so overcome with astonishment and terror that he could not move.

At her friendly voice he recovered from his fear, filled pockets and hat with the coins, bowed low and reverently, left the magic chamber, and hurried back to his cottage—and the sun rose on two happy people. Every anniversary of the day they went to the ruins to thank the fairy, who, however, ever afterward remained invisible.

The Key Fairy of the Günstersburg.

AT midnight, when the moonlight rests on the rustling oaks, or the winter snow glitters and winds howl, there rises a white form from the ruins of this robber Schloss, a wreath of flowers around the head, and in the girdle a bunch of keys.

Centuries ago a convent stood near, and a monk belonging to it, longing to possess some of the treasures of the underworld, was once bold enough, as the bells rang midnight, to climb to the spot where the fairy dwelt.

He used the formula employed to open the gates of the spirit-world, and instantly, white as a swan, rose the virgin beautiful to behold.

" What dost thou desire?" she asked.

The monk approached her too boldly, begging for the jewels of the depths, and she gave him such a blow with her keys that he fled in terror, and never dared to visit the place again.

Soon after, as a shepherd was feeding his sheep on a meadow near, a blooming, quiet maiden came and gathered flowers, which she bound in a garland; approaching him, and looking kindly at him, she let a flower fall. He picked it up and put it in his hatband.

The maiden departed smiling, but beckoned him to follow her.

Soon they reached the summit of the Güntersburg.

They entered a subterranean passage, a door opened, and the youth beheld the wonders of the fairy-world. Gold and precious stones glittered in the soft starlight that illuminated the vaulted chambers.

"Take what thou wilt," said the fairy; "but choose wisely."

He filled his pockets with gold and costly jewels, but in his rapid movements the flower fell from his hat. He looked around seeking the door and rushed out, hearing only the words, "Forget not the most beautiful treasure," and never stopped till he had reached the meadow and his sheep. He emptied his pockets of the precious treasures, when lo! they were worthless stones.

Legend of the Devil's Mill.

THE summit of the Ramberg, or Victor's Höhe, is strewed with gigantic ruins of the primeval rocks, and is called the Brocken of the Unterharz*

Two huge granite boulders, lying as if they had been placed there by hands, are the remains of the Teufelsmühle.

At the base of the mountain, in the ages long ago, a miller possessed a windmill.

But the mill, an inheritance from his great-great-grandfather, was in a tumble-down condition, and when the wind blew from the north or west the sweeps

* Unterharz—Lower Harz. The Brocken is in the Oberharz—Upper Harz.

stood motionless, for mountain and forest intercepted the " breath of God."

Often the miller had sat on the summit of the mountain, and thought how nice it would be if the mill only stood there in the free, full breeze, with a strong tower, built from the materials that lay scattered around in superfluous abundance.

Once, as he sat and mused in the twilight, the bats and owls just beginning their nocturnal rounds, a huge, swarthy labourer suddenly appeared before him, greeted him with a *Gott-sei-bei-uns!* and told him he would build him a mill, as soon as the miller signed a promise with blood to be his in thirty years.

Want, avarice, and vanity won the day with their unholy counsel, and the bond was signed.

Suddenly scores of little black figures issued forth from the darkness of the night, and began to work among the rocks; trees were cut down with a stroke, chisel and hammer rang on the granite, and the work went forward with the rapidity of enchantment.

The fear of the miller rose to despair, and as he saw the roof and the huge sweeps set up and finished, and the last millstone rolled to its place, he seized it with the power of a deadly terror, threw it from the rollers with such force, that it rolled down the mountain.

Then the black wings of the arch-fiend unfolded and spread themselves, he soared high in the air, let fall the millstone on the miller, who was buried beneath it and the ruins of the mill, broken to atoms.

The Origin of the Rammelsberg Mine, near Goslar.

THE rich treasures of the Rammelsberg were discovered in 970, according to tradition, by accident.

Otto the Great hunted in the forest. His squire Ramm dismounted, tied his horse to a tree, and went after some game that had been shot. The impatient animal pawed and stamped, and his rider returning, found a glittering piece of silver ore laid bare.

Another story is, that the discovery was made by a servant-girl in the mill at the base of the mountain.

She arose one morning before daybreak, and went out to gather wood, when she saw a fire burning on the mountain. She hurried to the spot, and found several men with white beards sitting around it.

Approaching them, she asked permission to take some of the burning coals to kindle her fire.

They gave no answer, but sat motionless, and gazed upon the ground.

At last she took some coals, saying to herself, " No answer means yes," carried them home and laid them on the hearth, but they would not burn. This she repeated several times, but the coals, once thrown on the hearth, refused to burn.

At last it became broad day, and a great heap of gold lay on the hearth, and on the spot where she had

seen the fire, lay only pebbles.   Search was made,
and the wealth of the mountain discovered.

A similar tradition, with slight variations, is told
of the *Burgmühle,* or castle mill, near Aschersleben,
on the Wolfsberg.

The tradition is quite as probable that Askanas,
grandson of Noah, died on the Wolfsberg in 1964
after the Creation, having left the East a few centuries previous, to escape idolatry.

Legend of the Hoppelberg.

MANY and mighty tribes—as the Wenden, Katten,
and Sassen—once dwelt in the Harz.

Bloody battles have been fought for the possession
of this district, whose dense forests and impassable
valleys afforded not only defence, but the pleasures
of the chase.

We find proofs of their existence here in huge
mounds filled with human skulls and bones, and in
the names of some of her villages, as, for example,
Dorf Kattenstedt.

These primeval mountaineers were most disturbed
by a wild and powerful monastic tribe of giant size and
strength, who frequently broke into the mountains,
plundered their huts, murdered children, women, and
old men, and led away the strong men into slavery.

Sometimes they only came in small numbers, but
the terror of their name went before them, and

caused the inhabitants, despite their peculiar bravery, without opposition, to flee into the ravines and caves, while the enemy took possession of all they could lay hands on.

One called these giant people the Huns. No other race possessed such immense size and terrible strength. They were held to be unconquerable, and mighty magicians. Nevertheless, it happened that once when a body of these giants broke into these mountains, the bravest of the inhabitants united in defence against them ; clad in steel, with shield and spear, they marched to meet the advancing foe.

The Huns, surprised at opposition, and the sight of the huge weapons of the mountaineers, hesitated to begin the attack.

Then the king of the Huns came forward and cried, in scorn, " Do you fear these dwarf figures ? Tarry here ; I alone will fight their whole army, which extends itself beyond our view. As the storm-wind breaks in pieces the trees of the mountains, so shall these fall before my strong arm."

He seized his lance and battle-axe, hurled his javelin into the thickest ranks of the enemy, his arrow to that point where their leader stood, and stormed after them down the hill like a rock suddenly broken from the mountain's side, crushing and destroying all on his way, defending himself against the cloud of arrows that met his advance with his huge shield.

His followers remained on the summit of the hill

and followed with flashing eyes their hero king, that they might be ready to hasten to his aid if in danger.

The crashing of his sword, as it rent helmet of oak and coat of mail, resounded above the wild cry of the combatants and the clashing of shields.

Unceasing was his way through the ranks, and dying and maimed marked his path. At last he reached the spot where the commander stood surrounded by his braves, and here his progress was arrested.

Stubborn is the conflict; surrounded and shut in, his position seems terrible ; and the onlooking Huns cry out, " Shall we hasten to his aid ?"

And others answer, " No, no ; he would be enraged if we deprived him of the glory of being the sole conqueror. But see ! see ! The enemy grows weak ; now he totters; our king wields more quickly, more mightily his arm ! They sink ! They fly ! Victory ! Victory ! Great is the glory of our tribe, and of our mighty champion."

They raise the song of triumph, and march to meet the royal conqueror, who leans upon his spear, and looks upon his advancing army without going forward to receive it.

He gives them a sign ; they raise his helmet and loosen the coat of mail; and the hero sinks lifeless on his bloody shield.

Strong and deep is the sorrow of his people, and loud are the lamentations of woe.

At length one of the elders of the tribe exclaims " Why do we lament the fallen ? Is not death the, destiny of all, and is there a more glorious death than that of the conqueror in the hour of victory? Let us make a grave for our king on the field of his victory, a grave that shall not only receive his ashes, but proclaim his victory to the most distant centuries."

And they did so. They made a funeral pile, and laid the victor, borne upon his shield, upon it, and the Huns formed a circle around the burning wood and sang the death-song, led by the bards.

" The people shall see their king no more. And the halls of his palace must remain forever desolate. Never again shall the people hear his voice, but in their hearts he shall dwell forever."

The flames grow less, the death-song ceases. In silence they gather the ashes in the sacred urn, lay the shield upon the ground, the urn upon it, and his armour above it.

Many lay upon the sacred heap what is held most dear, hunting spear or battle-axe. And now the whole tribe sets hand to the work.

" We will build," they said, " a grave which neither man can destroy nor storms and tempests wash away."

And they heaped rock on rock, and levelled whole hills to the plain to pile up the giant grave to a giant king, and called it the Hero's Grave.

And that is the *Sargberg*,* or Coffin mountain.

---

* This mountain has the form of a coffin, which may account for the origin of the name.

The White Lady.

THE Blakenburg family ghost is called the White Lady. A portrait bearing this name hangs in the castle, said to be a likeness of a Countess of Orlamünde. The legend is as follows :

The Earl Otto von Orlamünde died in 1340—several dates are given—and left a young and beautiful widow, Agnes by name, a duchess by birth, and the mother of two little children, a son of three, and a daughter of two years.

The widow lived alone in the Plassenburg, and thought often it were better to marry again.

One day a remark of the Earl, Albert the Handsome von Nürnberg was repeated to her : " I would willingly espouse the fair Countess Agnes, but for the four eyes."

The Countess fancied he meant her two children. Seeing they stood in the way of her marriage, she resolved to free herself of them, and engaged a man named Hager, with promises of rich gifts, to murder them.

The murderer is said to have confessed his crime on the rack. According to another tale, the Countess murdered them herself by sticking pins in their sculls.

Her guilty spirit cannot rest, but wanders in Orlamünde and Blakenburg. Her appearance always betokens death in the family.

Frau Berta is also called the White Lady. She haunts the imperial royal palaces, and also Darmstadt and Carlsruhe.*

As family ghost she harms no one, greets every one she meets, never speaks, and always wears a white veil and carries a bunch of keys in her girdle.

The Chapel of Roses.

IT was a stormy, dismal winter night, when a teamster drove with a heavy load of wine along the almost impassable road near the little mountain church of Elend,† at the foot of the Brocken.

The disc of the moon blinked only seldom through the dark clouds, which, restless, and ever succeeded by new ones, chased each other across the heavens.

A sharp north wind shook the bare branches of the trees that grew thick on both sides of the way, blew the snow into the ravines, and heaped it into huge snow-drifts, which threatened the traveller unacquainted with the locality with danger.

The wind grew every moment more sharp and cutting, the snow deeper, and the difficulty greater for the tired horses to draw their weary load.

Often the teamster stood and listened, and gazed into the darkness in search of some shelter, and called for help, and heard the echoes of his own voice ring deep in the snowy wood, but all remained desolate, dumb, and awful.

* *Carls*, Charles ; *Ruhe*, rest.   † *Eland*, pronounced Aylend.

No bark of a dog that so rejoices the nightly wanderer, no lowing or neighing of friendly stall.

The silence of death reigned; only now and then the dark wings of some nocturnal bird of prey fluttered over his head, and a ghostly rustling was heard among the dry underbrush; the stars seemed like silent, cold eyes looking down on the weary man and horses, the clouds scudded silently past, and the snow, too, was silent as a spirit.

The lonely traveller grew more terrified, and urging on his horses, the waggon suddenly sank in a deep place, and no efforts of the tired animals could move it from the spot. Loud cried the deserted man for help. No one heard. In despair he wrung his hands and besought the Virgin to aid him in his distress.

Suddenly he heard a rustling in the thicket, and a female form, like the silver moon when she appears above the peaks of the mountains, glided out of the darkness into view, slender as the fir-tree of the Hartz, rosy as the early dawn, fresh as meadow-dew, beautiful as eternal youth.

A lustre like a sunset in spring, or an Alpine glow* on the eternal snow, floated around the heavenly form, and breathed on the rigid snow masses a soft glimmer like a fairy light.

Terrified, the teamster gazed at the radiant Virgin, who with an enchanting, heavenly smile approached

*This *Alpenglühn*, or Alpine glow, on the eternal snows of the Alps, is gorgeous beyond the possibility of description, only the eye may picture its glorious majesty.

the sunken waggon, and with a single touch drew waggon and horses out of the deep place.

Surprised by the mysterious vision, and cheered by the unexpected aid, the teamster endeavoured to thank his helper and deliverer, and expressed his regret that he had neither cup nor goblet in which to offer her a draught of wine.

At these words the strange apparition touched a shrub that stretched forth its dried, thorny branches, when instantly leaves and buds burst forth, and soon the whole shrub was loaded with most beautiful roses, that breathed forth a wondrous and unwonted perfume.

The Virgin Mary, for it was she herself, broke off clusters of the roses and formed a drinking-cup, and as the teamster would return it filled with wine, the vision had vanished.

Meanwhile the horses had gone on with the waggon, which they now drew with perfect ease, but stood still before the chapel of Elend, and could not be brought from the spot.

The teamster entered with reverence the oratorium, to thank the Almighty for his deliverance, when lo! he recognized in the figure of the Virgin his deliverer, and placed the rose drinking-cup as a costly relic before her shrine.

With amazing rapidity the fame of the miracle of the Church of Roses spread over Germany, and it became one of the most frequented and sacred shrines.

The original of the rose-cup was sent to Rome; but first an exact copy of it was made in clay and preserved in Elend.

The most wonderful miracles continued to be performed; the devotees swarmed to the mountain church, so that it was enlarged, and seven doors were cut in its walls.

Princess Ilse.

THE beautiful Princess Ilse, daughter of King Ilsing of Schloss Ilsenburg, having ridden to the chase with her royal father, and her lover the Ritter Ralf, lost her way on the wild mountains, and came at nightfall to the gates of the fairy world, over which the Fairy Queen of the mountains rules. The Queen met her with kindness, and invited her to enter her gorgeous crystal palace.

Hesitating and with fear she followed the powerful sovereign; gnomes and cobolds attended everywhere with homage.

Beautiful Ilse tarried a whole year in the richly adorned subterranean world, witnessed the mysterious government, policy, and life of the fairies, the creations and destructions by the king of the giants, the hostile relations of the Fairy Queen to the Giant King, the unhappy loves of her children Rumar and Romar, and what she could not understand the amiable Queen explained to her, and introduced her fully to the fairy world.

But all the splendour and glory of this fairy realm could not still Ilse's longing for her beloved Ralf, and the light of the upper world.

She demanded her return, which her fairy Majesty granted, but threatened her with destruction should she ever reveal to mortal what she had seen.

Princess Ilse returned to the friendly light of day and rejoiced in the fidelity of her lover.

But he threatened her with the loss of his love if she did not tell him where she had been so long a time, and what she had seen.

The two lovers seated themselves on the soft moss. Ilse laid her lovely head upon Ralf's breast, and gazed up into his face with her wonderful and faithful eyes; Ralf laid his hand upon her shoulder, and beautiful Ilse began her tale.

With caresses she betrayed the secrets entrusted to her, and described the magnificence of the Fairy Queen.

The new moon rose and the stars appeared one after another in the dark-blue heavens; fair Ilse chatted on, related the legends of the Harz—of the giants and dwarfs.

Ralf listened at first in silent astonishment, and hung enraptured on the tales from her beautiful lips, then he began to dream and fancy, and at last fell asleep.

In the grey of the morning, as he awoke, he heard still the murmuring tones of the Princess, and as he

8

turned to salute the princely maiden, he saw, instead of Ilse, a crystal-clear bubbling spring illuminated with the dawn.

The water sprang gaily out of the soft moss, and murmured ever in a thousand leaps and tiny, water-falls over the moss-grown rocks adown the vale.

Deepest despair seized Ralf's spirit ; he knew now what he had done, and what had become of Ilse through her betrayed secret, a clear pure stream doomed for ever to ripple and murmur through the mountains.

Ralf built a cottage near the spring, and when the new moon rose Ilse awaited him by the mossy bank, leaned her head caressingly on his breast, and he heard her sweet prattle till the blushing dawn spread her radiance over the silver ripplets, and then the fairy virgin vanished in the blue air.

Princess Ilse and the Deluge.

PRINCESS ILSE, says another legend, in order to escape the general deluge, fled with her lover to the Brocken. But before they had reached that witch-haunted mountain, and just when standing on the rocky wall connecting the Ilsenstein with the Wester-berg, the rock on which they stood was rent asunder in order to separate the lovers, whereupon they both leaped together into the floods,

The Ilsenstein.

THIS lordly cliff and the Westerberg were once connected, it is said, by a granite wall, which was rent asunder by flood and storm from the Brocken; and according to one legend, Princess Ilse issues from the rock at dawn, when the weather is mild, robed in white satin, her long golden hair floating around her like a veil, a diadem of mountain crystal adorning her regal brow, lays aside her costly array, bathes in the crystal stream, and combs her golden hair.

Whoever is so happy as to meet her at the right moment, she calls with friendly voice, takes him by the hand and leads him before the Ilsenstein, which at her command opens, when she conducts him to her palace in the heart of the mighty rock.

There the most unheard-of splendour rivets his astonished gaze; the floors, walls, and ceilings glitter with gold, silver, and precious stones; the lofty arches are supported by columns of mountain crystal; while carbuncles illuminate the vast chambers with a soft light.

In the most magnificent of these chambers will the happy mortal find the most delightful entertainment; and when a youth, pure, and free from all guilt, bathes in the Ilse at the same time as the Princess, she will be free from the enchantment.

Whoever approaches her with impure heart, she

sprinkles with water, and instantly he turns into a fir tree.

> " *Es stehen der Tannen gar viele*
> *In ihres Bades Näh,*
> *Es hat sie atle verzaubert*
> *Die keusche Wasserfee!* "

> " And many a fir tree's deepest shade
> Falls o'er the crystal stream ;
> Enchanted by the pure mermaid,
> Their fate to moan they seem."

A Dream Under Princess Ilse's Firs.

IT was during the heat of August, when my friend Josephine and I sat long chatting on a moss-grown stone under Princess Ilse's dark evergreens.

Finally she went to gather some ferns and wild-flowers, and I fell asleep.

Then I heard a deep voice above me say, "I am Castiglione the magician. I approached the Princess Ilse with the guilt of falsehood on my soul, and she transformed me into the fir against which you are leaning. If she would only break the enchantment, and set me free, I would lead an honest, truthful life. Plead with her to release me."

"How can I do that?" I asked. "I never expect to see the Princess."

"Oh yes, you will. You will see her to-day."

Another voice joined in—" I am Booth, of Lincoln renown. People never knew what became of me. I came here to the Harz mountains, hoping to find favour with the noble Ilse after my heroic deed in freeing my country from a tyrant; but the Princess called my act murder, and I have been a sighing fir tree ever since."

"And you deserve it," cried Castiglione.

"Pull the beam out of your own eye, please," replied the infuriated Booth. "You dare to reproach me, you, who did not hesitate to add the last drop of an infant's blood to make your elixir of life? What insolence!"

I felt sure they would come to blows right over my head. Happily a melodious voice struck in, and interrupted the quarrel.

"I am Don Carlos, the unhappy son of Philip of Spain, and the victim of priestly bigotry. The Inquisitors gained my royal father's permission to make away with me, a son who loved him truly."

"I escaped, and History does not tell what became of me, simply because she does not know. I fled here to Princess Ilse for refuge, but I approached her at an unfavourable moment, and she transformed me into this spruce. If I could only be set free I would carry out my ideas of freedom."

"You are too late, my young friend," cried Castiglione. "Your ideas have been carried out. You don't seem to have kept up with the history of events. Bismarck has set the Germans free, and cleansed the moral atmosphere of the whole empire, sent the Jesuits adrift, and put a bayonet into the hands of every eighty men in a hundred to keep them out."

Here a deep sigh was heard.

" Oh, I am tired with standing so long ! Walking isn't half so fatiguing. Oh, how my back aches !"

" Who are *you ?*" cried Castiglione.

" I am the Wandering Jew. They keep up the story of my wanderings, but I have stood here in this tree for ages, shivering or roasting."

I felt quite bewildered, and almost afraid in the midst of this odd *Gesellschaft,** and shuddered as I thought more dreadful additions would speedily be made to it.

Suddenly a radiant form stood before me. Such beauty no mortal eye ever beheld outside of a dream. It was the Princess Ilse. Her long golden curls fell nearly to her feet, over a silvery-like robe almost transparent.

Her eyes were deep violet with an expression none could describe.

Above her milk-white regal brow glittered a diadem of brilliants and sapphires. Bracelets and rings of diamonds and pearls adorned her fair arms.

Extending her swan-white hand, with a ravishing smile, she said, "Come, I will show thee my home, my palace, and thou shalt dine with me."

We entered the Ilsenstein under a gigantic arch of mountain crystal ; a group of white-robed maidens met us, and attended us to the great throne-room.

*Society or company.

This was an immense chamber, lighted by a chandelier of brilliants hung in the centre, and single lamp-shaped rubies and carbuncles hung along the sides and in the corners.

The floor was of white and red roses, which were not crushed by the tread, but remained ever in rich fulness.

On each side of this regal chamber were sixteen colossal Norman arches, through which one saw, on the right advancing up it, a garden of every sort of fruit-trees, all bearing ripe fruits.

At the left, flowers of every clime. Fountains played, white-robed maidens moved among the fruit and flowers, or reclined on banks of violets and roses.

Soft music floated around us. Between each arch was a seat. Every seat was a bank of flowers, each different from the other.

Above each seat was a statue of a fairy of the Harz, alternately in mountain crystal and snowy alabaster.

At the upper end, under a majestic arch, stood Princess Ilse's throne.

The throne was one ruby, the canopy a single pearl, the steps leading up to the throne were emeralds.

Near the throne, in front of an arch, stood a table of silver, and two chairs of mountain crystal beside it.

The service was of gold, filled with the viands of the fairy world, and the choicest fruits and flowers.

A group of fair maidens sat in a rose arbour playing harp, lute, and harpsichord, while others stood by the table in attendance.

A pearl plate was handed us, and Princess Ilse herself poured the crimson wine into gilded crystal goblets bearing her monogram in diamonds and sapphires, touched her glass to mine, and saying, " I drink to thy happiness," she pressed her own glass to my lips, when lo ! I awoke, and there stood Josephine, poking a fern in my face.

" Oh, Josie ! " I exclaimed, "you can never know of how much you have robbed me with that stupid fern ! "

The Red-haired Trude.

AT a time when very few men lived upon the earth, when towns and villages were few and very widely separated, when there were no roads in the mountains, and before Romulus and Remus were rescued by the motherly wolf on the yellow Tiber, or Nausikaa fell in love with Odysseus, there stood a house on the site of Schloss Ilsenburg, inhabited by a widow and her daughter Trude.

Deeper in among the mountains stood an old stone Schloss on the granite wall connecting the Ilsenstein and the opposite-lying Westerberg, which had been bought, and was inhabited by a father and his fair daughter Ilse.

Nobody knew who the father was, but it was *supposed*—as people do in many cases—that he was some fallen and deposed Prince.

During the absence of the Prince and Princess Ilse

on a journey, a stranger, handsome and gay, without money, sack, or scrip, but rich in self-confidence and flattering words, sought hospitality of the widow and her daughter, and was warmly received and entertained.

Ralf "fell in love" with Trude, and a blissful summer was spent gathering wild fruits and flowers and hunting birds' nests among the mountains.

The nuptials were near, and the widow was busy with the bride's trousseau, when unexpectedly, with Autumn, arrived the foreign Prince and fair Ilse from their mysterious journey.

Ritter Ralf, it must be confessed, was very naughty. With an eagle-eye he perceived the radiant charms of Princess Ilse, and poor Trude was forsaken.

The widow reproached him with his perfidy, but he replied, "The eagle mates but with the eagle, and though I have fled from a severe father, I am of noble blood, and have found a *Braut* of my own rank."

The widow swore revenge, and consoled the weeping Trude, begging her only to wait till Walpurgisnacht * and her perfidious lover should be punished.

She made a league with the evil spirits of the mountains and the air, and devoted herself to the unholy arts of a witch.

Walpurgisnacht arrived, the widow stood on the

---

* Night before the first of May, when all evil spirits and witches, according to the legend, meet on the Brocken. See Goethe's "Faust."

balcony of her house and invoked the demons and witches, who swept through the night, which rested black as destruction on the mountains, heavy as the day of wrath and vengeance.

From the Brocken broke a terrible tempest. Awful thunders rolled, lightnings in fiery serpents cut their way through the heavens and mountains, and a tremendous flood swept down from the Brocken, destroying all in its course.

The coalers* clung to the rocky walls, but Princess Ilse looked calmly on the wild scene, saw the rocks rent on which her father's castle stood, and it, her lover, father, and servants all swept away ; and as she too was about to perish, a tall manly form, with majestic head and black locks—probably the Fairy King—seized her in his strong arms, wrapped her in a white mantle, and vanished.

Poor Trude, from the balcony by her mother's side, saw her faithless Ralf carried down the torrent, threw herself over after him, and when the flood had subsided the widow found them in each other's arms, washed up on the banks of the river.

* These coalers are charcoal burners. In the Harz and other mountainous districts of Germany, they dwell in little huts close by the scene of their labours. They frequently make an important and striking figure in the wild stories of those regions.

The Wild Huntsman.

EARL EBERHARD VON WÜRTEMBERG rode one day alone into the forest to amuse himself with the chase. Suddenly he heard a loud roar and noise, as of a hunter riding furiously past. He was terrified, dismounted in haste from his horse, and, approaching a tree, as if for defence, cried aloud to the imagined huntsman, asking if he intended violence.

"No," replied the now visible form of the hunter; "I am a man like thyself, and stand before thee quite alone. I too was formerly a noble.

"I found such pleasure in the chase, that I besought God to permit me to hunt until the judgment-day. Unhappily my sinful wish was granted, and for four hundred and fifty years I have hunted the same deer. But my race and name are known to no one."

Thereupon the ghostly hunter vanished.

Hans von Hackelberg, a master of the hunt in Brunswick, had an unhappy dream one night on the Harzburg. It seemed to him in his dream as if he struggled with a huge wild boar, which conquered him after a long combat, and that he died of his wounds.

He could not drive this terrible dream from his mind. Shortly after, he encountered a boar in the Harz similar to the one in his dream. He attacked him. The struggle remained long undecided. At length Hans conquered, and slew the animal. Rejoiced to see the boar stretched at his feet, he kicked the tusk with violence, exclaiming, " Thou shalt not yet kill me !"

But he had struck with such force that the sharp tooth pierced his boot and wounded his foot.

At first Hackelberg paid no attention to the wound, but continued the chase. On his return, however, the foot was so swollen that the boot had to be cut off. He hastened back to Wolfenbüttel, but the vehicle shook the foot so that he was obliged to stop on the way at Wülperode, where he died.

Before his death he expressed a wish that he might hunt for ever, and his wish was granted.

The Tut-Osel, or Tut-Ursel, always accompanies him.

At midnight, when in storm and rain, Hackelberg, with horse and dogs, tears through the Thuringian Forest, the Harz, and the Hackel Forest, the night or death-owl flies before him, which the people call the Tut-Osel.

The wanderer, when he hears the ghostly hunt, listens in terror to the barking of dogs, and hears the hu! hu! of the chase, and the uhu! of the death-owl.

In a Kloster in Thuringia lived, in the primeval days of convents, a nun called Ursel—Ursula—who always disturbed the choir of nuns by her howling singing; hence she was called Tut-Ursel. But after her death she disturbed them even more than in her lifetime, for at eleven every evening she poked her head through a hole in the church tower, and *tooted* dreadfully; and every morning at four she joined her voice in the matin-song.

For some days the holy sisters bore this lamentable disturbance; but at last, one morning, one of the nuns whispered in fear to her neighbour, "That is certainly the Ursel!"

Instantly the music ceased, their hair rose to mountains, and the nuns rushed out of the church screaming: "Tut-Ursel! Tut-Ursel!" And no punishment could induce a single nun to enter the church again until a Capuchin monk from a monastery on the Danube, noted for his sanctity, was summoned.

He condemned Tut-Ursel to banishment in the Harz, and to bear the form of a death-owl.

Here she encountered Hackelberg, and found as much delight in the hu! hu! of his eternal hunt as he in her uhu! and so they hunt for ever in company.

Another story is that the screech-owl is a nun, who was false to her vows, and left her convent to follow Hackelberg.

The origin of this legend belongs to the ancient pagan days. It is even disputed that a person called Hackelberg existed, and if so, the legend is ages older than the sixteenth century, the time when he is said to have lived.

The Wild Hunter—the Wanderer—was Wodan himself in the pagan days.

At the introduction of Christianity, we find a new

development of the ancient myths. Wodan becomes the foul fiend, then the godless Hunter, and the Wandering Jew. In the Black Forest, the eternal Hunter and the eternal Jew are regarded as the same person. They both always carry a Groschen in the pocket. In some parts of Germany the harrows are placed in the field with the teeth together, that the Wanderer may rest himself. According to some authorities, he may only rest on Christmas night, and then only when he finds a plough in the field; only on that he may sit down.*

Every seven years the Huntsman passes over the seven mining towns of the Harz, and woe to him who calls after him.

According to one legend, the Wild Huntsman met Christ at a river where He sought to quench His thirst, and would not permit Him to drink; he also drove Him from a cattle-trough; and when the Saviour found water in a horse's foot-print, and would drink there, he drove Him away. As a punishment, he is doomed to wander for ever, and eat only horse-flesh. This is the pagan legend Christianized. In West and South Germany we find the Wild Army. Odin, or Wodan, was the god, too, of armies, and always went out from Walhalla at the head of his ghostly array, while his nine Walküren conducted the fallen heroes back to Walhalla.

* The harrow and the plough shew his connections with *Wotan's* or *Wodan's* steed.

The Origin of the Philippine.

ONCE, long centuries ago, a Princess lived in Schloss Hohenstein who was very fond of almonds, but was firmly resolved never to marry, so she invented the following plan.

She caused every prince who came a-wooing—and her suitors were countless—to eat the half of a double almond, and she ate its twin half. And then she said, "If you can induce me to take anything from your hand without saying '*J'y pense,*' I am ready for marriage with you ; but if, on the other hand, I can lead you to receive any object from my hand without you repeating those saving words, you shall have your head shaved, and forthwith leave my . dominions."

But there was a trick in the stipulation, namely, the etiquette of the royal court forbade any person, on pain of death, to hand anything direct to the Princess, but rather to the lady-in-waiting, who presented it to her mistress.

But if the Kaiser's daughter chose herself to hand any one anything, who was there to forbid it ?

Thus it was for the luckless wooers a bitter sport, for let them exert themselves as they would to beguile the royal maiden into taking anything from their hands, the inevitable lady-in-waiting spoiled their sport,

But when Princess Huldigunde determined to get rid of a certain adorer, she grew so engaging that he became perfectly enchanted, and as he sat beside her, intoxicated with joy, she seized either a pomegranate, or an egg near her, and handed it to him, saying softly, " Keep this as a souvenir."

As soon as the wooer took the object, it sprang open, and a frog, or a hornet, or bat flew into his hair or face, and in his fright he forgot to say, *"J'y pense!"* And then he was shaved on the spot, and away with him.

This went on for years, and in all the kings' houses princes wore wigs. It happened at last that a foreign prince saw Huldigunde, and found her fair, and saw through the trick.

A friendly fairy had given him an apple, which he was to smell once a year, when a prudent idea should occur to him.

Just at the time when he first saw Huldigunde, it was time to smell the apple ; he smelt, and it occurred to him that if he would win the game through give and take, he must neither give himself nor take anything from her.

He caused his hands to be bound to his girdle, went with his marshal to court, and declared his wish to eat almonds.

Huldigunde liked this Prince, and commanded almonds to be handed him. Then his marshal took them and put them in his mouth.

The Princess inquired why he carried his hands in his girdle.

He replied that the etiquette of his court was still more severe than at hers; it was not permitted him to take anything with his hands, only with his feet or head.

"In that way," cried Huldigunde, "we shall never settle the game."

Prince Otto only shrugged his shoulder, and replied, "Only when you graciously condescend to take something from my boots."

And the court stood aghast at the bold idea.

"Why did you come to Schloss Hohenstein with such a stupid etiquette?" cried the Almond Princess.

"Because you are so beautiful," cried Otto; "and if I cannot win you I can look at you."

So Otto remained at the castle, and Huldigunde liked him better every day. She tried daily to beguile him into setting a hand free with offerings of fruit, flowers, even her bracelet, but Otto nodded to his marshal, who received them.

Then she dropped her handkerchief; but Otto lifted it with the toe of his boot, and swung it carelessly to and fro, and she stooped and took it from his boot.

So a whole year passed away, and the Princess said to herself, "An end must be made of this matter." So she told Otto she had the best garden in the world, and proposed to show it to him the next day.

9

It was time for the Prince to smell the apple again, and a brilliant idea came to him.

As they entered the garden, Otto exclaimed, "It is wonderfully beautiful here ; and in order that we may accompany each other without any disturbing element, I pray my Princess to adopt the etiquette of my court, and permit her hands to be bound one hour ; then we shall both be secure, and nothing disagreeable can happen to either of us."

Huldigunde consented, and they walked side by side with their hands bound.

The birds sang, the sun shone warm and clear, and from the trees the red cherries hung down to their cheeks.

Huldigunde looked wishfully at the ripe fruit and cried, "What a pity you cannot pluck me any."

But Otto replied, "Want knows no law," took a cherry in his mouth and offered it to her. The Princess could only put her mouth to his to take the cherry, and when she had the fruit between her lips—and his kiss with it—could not at the moment say, "*J'y pense.*"

And Otto cried, "Good morning, Philippine!" drew his hands from his girdle, and threw them around her neck.

Graf Arno's Capture.

ARNO, the wildest and most powerful robber knight of the Harz, dwelt securely enthroned in his strong Burg, the Arnstein, which lay on the Felsberg like an eagle's nest, from whose strong walls the old eagle flew daily forth for robbery and murder. He and his castle were inaccessible; frequently, when the inhabitants of the neighbourhood had united to storm his nest, he had sent them home with bleeding heads, and each time punished them by making worse disturbance than before.

The citizens of the near-situated Aschersleben suffered most by these raids; for when in the sweat of the brow they had cultivated their fields, and rejoiced in view of the approaching harvest, Arno would swoop down like a bird of prey, and gather the rich grains and fruits into his barns; and when the wealthy merchants of Magdeburg, Aschersleben, and Nordhausen, reckoning how they could make what was worth fifty per cent. bring a hundred, travelled past, he took pity on their problem-solving souls, and relieved their weary brains of the difficult calculations and the burden of sales by carrying off their goods to his castle— sometimes, indeed, the merchants themselves, whose friends redeemed them with heavy sums.

Often he kidnapped maidens, and it was not at all unwelcome to him, as one day, while he lay in vain in wait for booty, a troop of young girls showed itself near the woods where he lay hidden.

It was then, and is still in some Harz villages, the custom on the wedding day of a youthful pair to lead the bride out upon a mountain or a meadow, where her friends seek to take from her the bridal wreath. Dancing and singing they follow the fleeing bride, who strives to keep her treasure as long as possible, hides behind hedges and underbrush, till at last they rob her of her wreath and carry it in triumph to the bridegroom.

It was such a bridal party that issued this day from the gates of Aschersleben to enjoy the fun after the fashion of their ancestors, for the fairest flower of Askania, Ida, a merchant's daughter, celebrated her wedding.

How her bridal veil and ribbons fluttered and shimmered in the wind and sun, as she in the joy of her heart, light of foot as a fawn, flew over the meadow, pursued by her laughing companions.

Shouts of merriment and scraps of song rang over the laughing landscape to the wood where Arno lay concealed, watching the charming scene.

"Little maiden!" thought he, "if no train of waggons comes that I prefer, I can take thee; that is not difficult, and costs no blood."

And as the train came near, and the bride, ever in advance, would hide in the thicket, he seized her and bore her pitilessly away. The other maidens searched long in vain, till at last they caught sight of the fleeing robber with his booty.

What consternation! what lamentations! Breathless they fled back to the town, proclaiming the dreadful news with loud cries.

All became uproar, women ran moaning through the streets, girls locked themselves in their rooms, as if the robber were behind them, the older citizens talked and reasoned, the younger swore revenge, and the members of the town council moved with solemn steps and imposing mien toward the town hall, where the walls of the dark council chamber should become silent witnesses of all the wisdom of their puffed-up pride and self-importance.

Evening came on, the council chamber was lighted; the palate of each worthy member of the council rebelled against the fatigue of a longer sitting, and at last the Bürgermeister raised his voice and addressed his colleagues: "It is necessary, honourable gentlemen, that we come to a decision, and as it has been proved, through reliable witnesses, that the robber of the bride is our dangerous neighbour, the Earl von Arnstein, and the crime has been committed within the territory of our town, and as such a crime is punishable with death, we sentence the said Arno to death by the hangman, do we not?"

"Yes, your worship!" cried the chamberlain.

"Of course!" said the syndic.

"Certainly!" echoed the town clerk.

"Certainly!" agreed every member of the council unanimously.

"If we take into consideration," continued the Bürgermeister, "how much damage the said Arno of Arnstein has caused, death by the sword is too mild. Shall he not die on the wheel, or be quartered?"

"Of course!" said the chamberlain, with a knowing nod.

"Certainly!" agreed the syndic.

"How wise!" cried one part of the councillors; "How just!" another.

"I am of opinion," resumed the Bürgermeister, "that the execution should take place immediately, before the said Arno does any more mischief."

"Of course! of course!" cried the assembly.

"But—but—a—" resumed his worship, hesitating and undecided, "we must first have the criminal in our power, and that is—not—so—easy a matter. Can any one offer advice as to what is to be done?"

Silence! All were dumb. At last one cried, "We must take him prisoner!"

"Quite right," voted the councillors; "he must be taken prisoner."

"That also is my opinion," said the Bürgermeister. "Nevertheless it—is—no—easy matter—to accomplish. We could march out at once with all the armed men we possess, and storm——"

"Yes, yes," cried the syndic, "we will storm the nest!"

"We will storm it!" exclaimed the town clerk, with a look intended to be brave.

"How wise! how heroic!" was the praise on every lip, while the Bürgermeister continued his interrupted address: "But we have already experienced the fact that the Arnstein is not easy to seize. *By force nothing can be done.*"

"No, by force nothing can be done!" echoed the assembly as one man.

"We might attempt to take him by strategy," continued the orator; "but Arno is cunning as a fox, and we should probably only expose our town to more robbery if he discovered that we were trying to waylay him."

"Certainly! certainly!" agreed every mouth.

"Hence I give it as my opinion," concluded the Bürgermeister, "that as force and stratagem would only bring upon us expense and danger, and the result is uncertain, that—that—a—that we allow the matter to rest as it is, and leave the criminal to the punishment of Heaven. Do you not think so, gentlemen?"

"Certainly, your Worship, certainly! How wise! how mild! how forbearing!" shouted the assembly.

The Bürgermeister rose with official dignity, dismissed his colleagues with a wave of the hand, and the exhausted councillors were in the act of retiring, when the unhappy bridegroom rushed breathless into their midst.

" What is decided ? " he cried hastily, and seized the syndic by the arm.

" What's that to you ?" growled that dignitary, who felt himself insulted by such familiarity. " How do you dare to force yourself unbidden into the council chamber ? "

" I beg your pardon, gentlemen," stammered the bridegroom, surprised. " I come to give you a capital piece of advice—the idea just occurred to me."

Every face grew long from assumed dignity.

" What! you will give advice ? You—to us ?"

But as the young man entreated them to hear him, the Bürgermeister permitted him to speak, provided he would be short.

The bridegroom unfolded his plan, which, though unwillingly, was approved of.

Meanwhile, Arno concluded that his robbery of the bride was undiscovered, and was strengthened in this idea, as some days after he saw a group of maidens, decked in bridal array, issue forth from the town to the same meadow.

Suddenly he resolved to carry off one of them, and when they had danced themselves weary and had thrown themselves down on the grass to rest, he rushed out of the wood, and, like a vulture, swooped down upon his prey.

But, to his astonishment, the maiden, instead of resisting, held him fast, and the others drew forth daggers and attacked and killed his retainers. Resistance was useless; he could not free himself from the powerful arms of the disguised soldier. They dragged him to Aschersleben, and shut him up in a cage, where he starved to death.

The bridegroom put on Arno's armour, and the troop, concealed in loaded waggons, were conducted to the Arnstein by the disguised bridegroom. The warder saw the train approaching, and at once opened the gates to admit it.

Too late, when all were within the walls, he discovered his error. Soon they had possession of the stronghold, and the bride was restored to the bridegroom.

The cage they still show in Aschersleben, and the meadow is still called the Dance meadow.

There is a tradition of another knight of Arnstein, who, cold and cruel to all who in the least displeased him, was buried in the now ruined chapel. His ghost still haunts the ruins.

His second wife, a cruel step-mother, who oppressed her beautiful step-daughter, keeps him company. She is the spinner of the Arnstein, doomed to spin on till her web breaks, when her spirit will be set free.

Whether the ghostly monk bore relation to this cruel pair we are not told. He visits the ruins, probably nightly, but can only be seen every seven years by those who were born on St. John's Eve. His duty is to chastise idle and deceitful servants.

The Pebble.

A N old, poor, but honest man left his cottage to gather sticks and healing herbs in the wood for sale in the neighbouring town.

He soon had a huge bundle of sticks bound together for his weary, bent back—bent from the burden of toil and of years—and a luxuriance of the healing woodroofs made gathering them a light task ; but when he reached the town everybody said, " What's the need of wood now, when it is summer ?"

And the apothecary declared, " It is June, and the blossoms have already absorbed all the strength of the plants. You must bring them henceforth in May."

No one had an ear for the entreaties of the distressed man, and he set off for home hopeless and discouraged. He saw no way of deliverance out of his deplorable condition, no relief for his suffering wife. "Yes," he sighed, " if the bell in Wimmelburg had not been melted in the last fire, the bell through which God, the good Father, cured every sick person who heard its tones, there might be help for my poor wife ; or, if it is not all a fable, of the great treasure which the monks buried in Sittichenbach, and we could find it; or, if it is true about the hidden treasure in Eisleben, that only he can find who can watch four-and-twenty days and nights without closing his eyes. Oh ! I could watch the time, for sorrow keeps me awake every night. But all these tales must be only fancies, and the benevolent fairies in these mountains, who used to help the poor when they were near despair, are most likely long since gone, or else my trouble would have brought them to my relief. And with men, oh! with men there is no pity!"

It seemed to him, during these reflections, as if a long, giant, shadowy form brushed past him in the twilight, whispering in his ear, "Do not despair."

He looked up, but saw nothing save the shadow of the oak under which he sat, heard nothing save the sighing of the evening wind in its branches.

With a tear in his eye, he took the bundle of wood on his back and went on. A moment after he saw a shining object on his path. "Ei! what a beautiful pebble!" he thought. "I will take it home for the children to play with."

It was already late when he reached his cottage, and mother and children were asleep. The thought of their distress when they awoke caused him to try what he could do in the village, but all were deaf to his entreaties. It was a very dark night, and returning home from the village and opening the cottage door he almost sank down from terror, for it was light as if the house were on fire. He opened the door leading into the court; there it was as if all were in flames. He stood astonished, and gazed at the wonderful light, observed the direction whence it came, and perceived it came from the little room in which he had laid the pebble on the window bench.

He recollected the stone he had picked up, and the belief in a good mountain spirit, and hurried to the room·

The varied splendid colours of the pebble quite dazzled his eyes; he wrapped it in a cloth and hastened to his neighbour Bergmann, who knew all the stones of the Harz, and showed it to him.

Bergmann examined it well, and said, "I don't know this stone, but it must be worth money. Come with me to-morrow to the town, and if you only get a Thaler* for it, it is some help."

The following day they went to a jeweller, a Jew, and offered him the stone. Hardly had he cast eyes on it than he started, and cried, "Wonderful! How did you come by the stone?"

The poor man was so frightened he was unable to reply; but Bergmann, who had more experience, said, "It does not matter where the stone comes from ; you need only tell us how much you will give for it."

"Well!" replied the Jew, "shall I have it for a hundred Thaler?"

"How much?" cried the finder, who could hardly believe his ears. "I am not in a mood for jokes; say honestly how much you will give."

"What, did I say a hundred Thaler?" replied the Jew, for he thought the apparent anger of the seller had another cause. "I beg pardon; I meant to say a thousand Thaler."

* A Thaler is equal to three Marks, a Mark has the value of a shilling. The Franc of France, the Lire of Italy, and the Mark are nearly equal in value.

The two friends were speechless with astonishment; Bergmann, however, answered, "How could you make us such an offer? Give us the stone, for you will not pay what it is worth."

"Indeed you are right," said the Jew with a low bow. "You must be joking with poor Levi, for you must know I could not command a sufficient sum to buy so costly a jewel."

The amazement of the two friends increased every moment, for the Jew was known to be one of the richest men in the place. Bergmann, however, replied with caution, "You have guessed it; we only make a joke of the matter, and came really to beg you to recommend a purchaser."

"Why should I not?" replied the jeweller. "But as true as I am an honest Jew, there is only one person in the whole German Empire that could purchase the jewel, and that is Fugger* in Augsburg."

"And how high do you value it?"

"Well," said Levi, after having put his spectacles again on his nose, and examining the stone carefully, "if I am to give my honest opinion, it is worth three kingdoms."

The finder almost lost his equilibrium, while Bergmann put his hand to his head to see if it stood in the right place. "Three kingdoms, did you say?"

"Three kingdoms; and the purchaser could make money in the transaction."

An hour after the two friends stood before the

* Pronounced Fooger.

treasurer of the Prince, for the finder could not make up his mind to undertake the journey to Augsburg until he had provided for his wife and children, and asked him if he would advance a hundred thousand Thaler on the jewel, till they could sell it to Fugger.

But the treasurer was a vicious and avaricious man, who resolved to have the stone at any price, even by force if necessary, and as the friends would leave him, he threatened to throw them into prison if the stone were not delivered to him as his property for the hundred thousand Thaler.

To prevent unpleasantness they consented, and went home laden with gold.

Mother and children were provided with every comfort, and soon after went to live in Aschersleben, for they could not be happy among people who had refused assistance in their need, but fawned upon them now they were become rich.

The Jew received a handsome sum, and Bergmann was independent for life through his grateful friend.

But how did matters go with the dishonourable treasurer?   His punishment was swift and terrible.

The next day he broke a piece from the stone, the tenth part of it, and presented himself before the Prince.

"Your Highness has given me a command to purchase jewels, as precious and costly as were to be found, that you might present them to the Princess of the adjoining dominions, and thereby win her hand and realm.

" I have not been able to find anything costly enough, and hence only one thing remains to be done. I possess a stone of priceless value, an heirloom of my family, which one of my ancestors took from a Mahomedan Sultan. I will resign it, however painful it may be. Only look at it and judge if any female heart could withstand such splendour. The Princess will bestow her hand upon your Highness, and I only ask in payment a few towns and villages, and a thousand acres of forest, and a thousand acres of arable land. Judge if I am unreasonable."

" Thou shalt have it ; thou shalt have more than thy demand !" cried the Prince, as he beheld the glittering jewel, and embraced the treasurer, called him friend and brother, and commanded his secretary to draw up the documents giving the treasurer the half of his kingdom.

The treasurer went joyfully home, dreaming of princely honours, for had he not still a greater part of the stone in his possession ?

Meanwhile the Prince called his favourite courtiers and showed them the stone. No one spoke for astonishment. At last one of the surveyors of the mines remarked how wonderful it was that many pebbles possessed such brilliant colours, and it was to be regretted that they faded in a few days.

" What ? a pebble ? " cried the Prince.

" Yes, your Highness, only a pebble."

" A pebble ?   Not a precious stone ?   Then I have been deceived."

" Has your Highness bought it at a high price ? Such stones are found in the earth, but the sunlight soon fades the colours."

" I have promised the treasurer half my kingdom for the stone."

Command was given to arrest the treasurer, but a friend had given him warning, and he had fled. They pursued him, the Prince at their head, found the unhappy man, deceived as well as deceiving, in a tree, and shot him dead on the spot.

The Monk and the Spring.

IT was at Whitsuntide of the year 1292, as tradition tells us, that the town council of the free, imperial Mühlhausen issued a proclamation, that whoever could discover and conduct a spring into the upper town, which suffered much from fires through want of water, should be richly rewarded ; and in case he had committed a crime, he should be pardoned.

At that time a monk of Kloster Reifenstein sat in the dungeon of the Rabenthurm *—now called the Adlerthurm †—under sentence of death.

In the days of his freedom, when he had gone on

---

* *Rabenthurm*—raven tower.   †*Adlerthurm*—eagle tower.

affairs concerning his convent from Pfaffenrode to St. Daniel, he had often seen a spring among the hills.

The proclamation of the council penetrated to his criminal cell, and he recalled this spring to his memory, and felt a wild longing through it to regain his freedom.

But the spring bubbled up in a deep valley, and a long chain of hills lay between it and the town.

And the monk thought and studied, for before his soul stood the fragrant dishes of his convent and the costly wines, as attractive as the fleshpots of Egypt to the Jews; but with this vision stood the hangman, hand-in-hand with the impossibility of moving this spring through these hills, grinning in diabolical glee.

He tossed restlessly on his bed of straw, longing for the dawn.

Now he sank into an uneasy slumber, disturbed by the most frightful dreams. The Rabenthurm seemed to quake and tremble, he heard distant thunder, and saw the glare of the lightning.

Now the foul fiend stood by his miserable bed tempting him.

In exchange for his soul, he promised to conduct the water of the spring to the upper town, and produced a roll of parchment containing a plan of the work.

At length the unhappy man consented to the proposals.

Again he dreamed of his childhood, of his dead

10

mother, of the fields and woods where he gathered the first daisies and violets of spring ; and now again he listened to the raging storm.

At break of day the monk opened the fatal roll Judge of his astonishment and joy, as he saw the way marked out over hills and through ravines, by which the spring could be conducted with little difficulty to the place required.

He immediately made his proposals to the council·

His freedom was promised him if the work succeeded, and a body of labourers was given him for the carrying out of his plan.

And soon the crystal stream gladdened the thirsting upper town with an abundance of water.

But the monk, so soon as he had fulfilled his contract, disappeared, and even gratitude could find no trace of him.   He was never seen again.

Hildegard and the Hainerburg.

IN the thirteenth century there lived in Mühlhausen a respectable locksmith, who was also an alderman.

This Herr Adam had six sons and an only daughter, Hildegard, who was the loveliest maiden of all the plains of Germany.

The father's pride and joy were in these children, but his happiness was doomed to annihilation.

A wild and lawless knight of the Castle Hainerburg surprised Hildegard alone at home, her father and brothers being absent in the terrors of a fire in the city, and carried her off in a deadly swoon to his castle.

Inexpressible rage filled the hearts of the citizens at the news of this violence, and they agreed to unite in the coming week for the destruction of the castle.

But the father, distracted with grief, determined at once to rescue his child.

The very next night, the Ritter of the Hainerburg being absent on some villainous scheme, the father, with his six sons, knelt in the church of the Virgin, and besought her aid in his bold project.

And the petition was heard, for midnight was hardly past before the knights left behind in the Burg had been overpowered by the strong arms of the avengers of innocence, and thrust into the deepest dungeon.

They prayed again for strength; and now the walls and towers fell thundering in the moat, for the Virgin had appeared on the battlements, encouraging them, and their strength had become superhuman.

And when morning dawned, the sun illuminated only a shapeless mass of ruins, and on the ruins the conquerors knelt and thanked heaven for the given strength.

Great were the jubilee and gratitude of the citizens when they saw the fallen fortress, and great their praise of the victors.

The fair Hildegard retired to the Brücken Kloster,

where she died ; and still the maidens of Mühlhausen
sing many a song of her beauty and singular fate at
the joyful dance of the *Kirchweihfest.**

The Three Stone Partridges.

ON a flying buttress of the colossal Marienkirche,
in Mühlhausen, are three stone partridges, and
I am about to explain to you how they came there.

At the time when Germany was in the middle of
the great Reformation contest, two prelates sat together with their well-filled—for the empty ones
were speedily filled—wine-cups before them, and dis-
cussed the *pros* and *cons* of the Reformed doctrines,
and whether Mühlhausen was likely to adopt the
Lutheran creed.

At last one of the reverend prelates grew angry,
and exclaimed: " Those three partridges now turning
on the spit in the kitchen will fly, before the faith of
the heretical Augustine monk will gain power in this
good city."

But, lo ! scarcely were the haughty words uttered,
when a cooing and a fluttering of wings were heard.

The prelates fled in affright, seeing themselves robbed
of their dinner. The partridges flew forth and settled

* In Germany an annual festival is held in commemoration of the
dedication of the church of the place, called the *Kirchweihfest*—
dedication festival. Feasting, dancing, and universal merriment
are the order of the day. Friends are invited from far and near
and it is an occasion of general re-union in the parish.

on a buttress, where they were turned to stone, and remained as heralds of the dawn of a better day.

✻

The Forester and the Enchanted Castle.

THE forester of *Scharzfels,** with his gun on his shoulder, was one day sauntering through the wood, when, as he turned a corner, he saw three men in a young plantation, digging, and thereby doing much mischief.

Already a strong oath was on his lips as the figures turned round, and, through their odd, foreign appearance, frightened back every expression of anger.

One was a tall—from the weight of years not much bent—grey-headed old man. His bald head, from which, on each side, short silver locks hung down; a long white beard falling over his breast; the lean, stern features, and the black robe, gave him the appearance of an anchorite.

The second was a strong, powerful youth, with flaming eyes. An odd-shaped pointed hat rested on his curly black hair, and an uncultivated beard covered the lower part of his face.

The third was a noble, imposing form—the fearless countenance framed in a thousand auburn locks of curly hair; the eye was full of fire and courage; the bold lips full of power.

All three looked at the approaching huntsman with

---

* The ruins of this castle are among the most imposing in these mountains.

so much firmness and composure that he was only able to inquire: " What are you doing here, gentlemen ?   You are trampling under foot the young growths ; and with your scraping and digging, you will destroy many a thriving tree."

One of the strangers replied to this address mildly ; regretted that they had certainly caused a little damage, but that was unfortunately not to be prevented, since they sought just on this very spot certain stones which were absolutely necessary to them, and that they were come from a great distance to make the search.

They expressed themselves, however, willing to make indemnification, if the forester would only make his demands.

A further conversation betrayed to the forester that the strangers were Venetians, and the result of it was that he permitted them to depart without hindrance, or without accepting the smallest indemnity.

Several years passed away ; but every St. John's Day the forester saw and spoke with the same three strangers.

At last, one sultry summer afternoon, he threw himself down under a tree, and soon sank into a deep sleep.

How long he had slept he could not tell.   As he opened his eyes he saw himself in a perfectly strange place, in which, directly before him, rose a stately, wonderful castle, surrounded by a high wall.

Terrified, the forester gazed around. It was certain that he had never before seen the neighbourhood, and that he had been transplanted from Scharzfels to the spot by enchantment.

In the anguish of his spirit he said the Creed, the Lord's Prayer, the *Ave Maria*, prayers for storms, and all the others he could think of, all mingled in the wildest confusion, like one who had taken leave of his senses.

But whether it was that he had left out a word, or was not earnest and devotional enough, the castle and its enclosing walls stood immovable.

The terrified man knew of nothing better to do than to resign himself to his fate, and to observe more closely his surroundings.

Dark cypresses rose behind the stone walls, and fig trees thrust their wonderfully crooked fingers forward, as if they would draw him in; shining lizards crept up the wall, glanced at him with their glittering eyes, and then wriggled hurriedly into the garden, which he could see through a grated gate under a great arch.

Behind and among the shrubbery and trees he could see all sorts of marble figures; goat-footed heathen gods, making awful faces; small hump-backed dwarfs with cocked hats; hunters with puffed-out cheeks blowing the horn; ladies with farthingales and horse-heads; urns around which salamanders, dragons, and other poisonous worms, with open jaws and red tongues, dragged their slimy lengths; and many other indescribable, diabolical objects.

Among all these grinning creatures strutted a pea-cock, in which certainly pride made a most ridiculous figure, as he craned his beautiful neck in the brilliant sunlight, and dragged his gorgeous tail—alas! by means of the ugliest feet and legs ever made.

Suddenly the gilded, grated door flew open, an old Moor came out, bowed low before the forester with his hands meekly crossed before him, invited him by a wave of the hand to follow him, and both entered the garden.

Intoxicating clouds of perfume floated toward him from every bush and hedge.

Wonderful, never-before-seen flowers nodded to him in greeting from their slender stalks, and bent before him their lovely heads.

Brilliant birds flew from branch to branch before him, and sang with almost human voice.

Then an ugly sea-cat threw itself down from some tree, with its winding tail twisted around some branch, ground the teeth with a horrid grin, and sprang back into the thick foliage.

From a side path a purple stork came forward with solemn gravity, twisted the long neck up and down to affected compliment, scraped with his thin legs behind him, and then walked resolutely before the forester and the conducting Moor, looking almost constantly back to see if they were following.

In one of the marble basins a stone vintager upset continually the cask, and the clear, foaming new wine that streamed from the bung-hole bubbled up in the face of the sipping boy; in another an idol, ending in a fish's tail, blew out of a shell the clear stream in the air, and the dust of drops shone in the light like diamonds and rubies. White temples with ivy-entwined pillars glittered behind the hedges.

The forester followed like one in a dream, resisting, yet drawn on by an irresistible, enchanting power, until they reached a colossal castle, built in a style perfectly unknown to him.

He climbed a marble flight of steps, and went on over costly carpets, so soft and smooth that he could not hear his own steps.

The fragrance of balsamic spices floated delightfully on the air from censers in every chamber.

Richly-worked tapestry covered the walls, the softest cushions invited to repose, the light, like a soft twilight, fell through green windows, and composed the spirit to a sweet calmness and peace.

From the lofty ceiling rare birds warbled their delicious melodies in golden cages, and a grey parrot sat on his perch and pecked with his crooked bill the golden wires of his hated cage.

Here the Moor stood still, threw open a folding-door and pushed the benumbed forester into a great *salon*.

In this vast chamber he stood fascinated, like one

under enchantment, and gazed upon the extraordinary objects on every side. Around the costly chamber, near the magnificent walls, stood all sorts of animals in life-size, in beaten gold, a perfect imitation of nature. Amazed, the forester gazed at the beautiful forms. He never could have satisfied his eyes with looking ; and who knows how long he might have stood there, if through another door the three men had not entered whom he had so often seen near Scharzfels ?

They approached him, pressed his hand in the most friendly manner, and enquired how the chamber pleased him, and which piece he would choose.

After he had expressed his astonishment at the way he had been introduced into the castle, the forester, in reply to the question as to what object he should prefer if permitted to choose, said he would unhesitatingly select the stag with the beautiful antlers.

After some conversation, the eldest of the three said : "You have known us many years, and are aware that we went frequently to Scharzfels to search for metals and stones, which you stupid Germans do not prize, but which are, notwithstanding, of great value. We have now sufficient wealth, but we would wish to thank you for your forbearance, and entertain you as an honoured guest."

The forester was conducted to a *salle à manger* glittering with gold, silver, and crystal. The rarest exotics beautified the table, and stood in graceful baskets and vases in every part of the apartment.

The most delicious viands and oldest wines were served, and not till a late hour did the merry party seek repose. The forester sank, in his silken couch, quickly into the arms of friendly sleep.

On awaking he looked in surprise around him, for he lay under the shady beech in full view of Schloss Scharzfels.

"What a droll dream !" he cried, springing up and brushing the grass and moss from his clothes. But he stood as if transfixed, as he beheld the stag he wished for—the golden stag with great diamond eyes—lying in the grass beside him ! The three men he never saw again, not even on St. John's Day.

The Steinkirche* and the Hermit.

IN the grey days long ago, when paganism ruled the land, there stood on the hills near the cave called the Steinkirche—altars to the gods.

Bright were the fires to Krodo in the darkness of the night, and on the opposite cliffs rose the fire pillar in honour of the goddess Ostera.†

The crackling flames illuminated the country and the mountains, and invited the inhabitants of the near-lying vales and heights to the wild customs, the bloody sacrifices, and the raving dance of heathenism.

* *Steinkirche*—stone church.
† From *Ostera* we have the name Easter.

Then came from a southern land a hermit to this district. He beheld the smoking sacrificial altars, he heard the songs of the reeling, staggering heathen, and with a slow and solemn tread he climbed the mountain.

The peculiar, reverence-awaking appearance of the stranger produced quiet among the raging throng. One seated himself here, another there, another leaned on his spear, and all listened in silence and attention to what the strange figure might have to say to them.

And as the tempest with hollow moans and wails sweeps over the tree-tops, so the aged stranger lifted up his voice, and preached to the assembly the Christian faith with ever-increasing enthusiasm.

At first they heard quietly his earnest words; but as he began to condemn the gods so dear to them, and challenged them to break in pieces their idols, and turn to the worship of the only true God, their rage kindled.

They sprang to their feet, forced him to silence, and after a short consultation voted unanimously that the blasphemer of their gods must die.

In a few moments the trembling old man was seized by the giant forms, and led down from the summit of the mountain to a place suitable for the execution.

The hermit sent up a petition to the Almighty for strength and courage in the trying moment, released himself from their arms with a Samson strength, seized from one standing next him a wooden battle-axe, and thus addressed the bloodthirsty multitude:

"So sure as I with this weak tool split this firm rock, so sure as this wood produces a temple for the worship of the one eternal God in this immovable mass of stone, so true is the word, the gospel, which I proclaim to you."

When he had uttered these words, he struck with trembling arm the rough cliff, and lo! the firm rock yielded like soft clay to the weak blow of the wooden axe!

And at this moment the sun shone forth from behind thick clouds, bathing rocks and wood with a warm, rosy light, and the birds in a thousand voices sang the praises of Creator and Father.

And the hearts of the wild Sassen* were opened; with one mind they sank on their knees in reverence and adoration before the God of the white-headed old man who had received the power to work such a miracle.

They vowed to a man henceforth to forsake the worship of Krodo, to remain true to the new faith, followed the venerable hermit to the banks of the Oder, and were baptized into Christ's death and resurrection, and from every side the people flocked to hear the words of the apostle.

Thus was formed in the rugged, steep cliff the primeval cave, the Steinkirche, the meeting-place of the first Christians of this neighbourhood.

*Sassen—Old German for Saxon.

The Nymph Ruma and the Weingarten Höhle.

IN the middle of fruitful fields and green meadows not far from Scharzfels rises the ball-shaped alabaster Römerstein, on whose summit ragged cliffs rise in the air resembling the ruins of a castle.

In the days before authentic history a race of giants dwelt hereabout, who, fearing the mountain-spirit,* piled up these cliffs and constructed thus a giant fortress, of which these cliffs are the proud remains.

Romar, a blooming youth of this race, was once hunting in a neighbouring forest for deer or wild boar.

The soft air fanned gently his glowing face, the birds sang in the thicket, and the gentle influence of the hour led him to slacken his pace.

Suddenly he stood still before a maiden asleep on a mossy bank under the rustling trees.

Silently admiring, Romar gazed at the sleeping beauty, and the sweetest emotions filled his breast, till the stranger opened her eyes and beheld him, uttered a scream of terror, sprang up, and fled into the thickest of the forest.

A moment Romar stood rooted to the ground; then coming to his senses, he followed the fleeing maiden, and, soon overtaking her, quieted her fears by kind and

* *Berggeist.*

honest words; and this first meeting gave rise to many others. All suspicion, every fear vanished, and love speedily filled the maiden's heart.

Romar inquired after the descent of his beloved, and turned pale as he discovered that she was a nymph, and the daughter of the Berggeist, so hostile to his race, and a river goddess, and dwelt in the neighbouring mountain lake.

The nymph reassured him, told him she was her father's favourite, and he had never refused her a single request, and certainly would not refuse his consent to their union

Accordingly, during the absence of the Berggeist, they were married.

A long time had passed, and Romar slept one day under an oak near Runa, who held a lovely boy in her arms. · Her father, returning from his journey, stepped out of the thicket, and came suddenly upon them.

His first glance at the pair told him what had happened, and a smothered tone of anger forced itself from his trembling lips.

Terrified, the nymph sprang up, and as she saw her secret discovered, and her father so enraged, she rushed toward him and entreated him to be calm. Romar now came forward and sought from the old mountain god reconciliation; but the latter only became more enraged.

A wave of his hand called whole troops of well-armed dwarfs together, who were commanded to lead away mother and child; while others so maltreated Romar, that he only escaped, covered with wounds, to the Giant Castle.

The Berggeist now tormented his unhappy daughter every hour to give up her husband. But her love for Romar only increased, and her father in his insane rage seized the child, broke it in pieces on the rocks, cursed and swore because he could not take the same measures with his mother, created with a wave of his hand the cave, the Weingarten Höhle, banished her into it, and left her with a laugh of scorn.

Banished into the earth, shut up in a cave, the entrance guarded by malicious cobolds, the wretched Ruma sought to reach Romar, and a succession of cavings in proves her efforts to set herself free; but her watchful father always thrust her back into the depths of the earth.

At last, after long years, she succeeded, by a subterranean way, in escaping from her father's dominions, as a full stream to spring into the light of day, and at a time when he, by the decree of an inscrutable destiny, had been attacked by a sort of torpor, she reached her old residence, the Nymph's lake, and was reunited to her faithful husband.

The river which springs from the mountain on the border of the Gyps Mountains is called, in honour of the faithful, loving nymph, the Ruma. Still its waters redden with the blood of her innocent child.

The cliffs of the ruinated Giant Castle wear mourning still, and bear the name of the hero, the Römerstein, or Römar's rock.

Legend of the Schildberg.

NOT far from the Lautenthal there existed in the pre-historic times the Schloss Schiltberg, or Schildberg, of whose builders, destroyers, and history we know next to nothing. All we know is that the Kaiser Frederic I., in war against Henry the Lion, took the castle in 1180.

On the rugged, precipitous rocks stand the ruins of a dilapidated tower, now half veiled by clouds and mists, now echoing the roar of the savage tempest.

Beneath, in the still valley, is a half-sunken grave, and a weeping willow spreads sadly her branches over it. Above, on the wild rocks, once stood a strong castle, whose walls hid many a deed of horror and crime. Below, in the peaceful vale, there was a small, simple hermitage, where an old hermit had dwelt alone long years.

From the high fortress the robber-band of knights rode down the mountain, for they perceived the long-desired prey in the distance.

Beneath, by the quiet hermitage, appeared the pious old hermit, looked reprovingly upon them, and shook his silver-white locks.

"Ye wild knights!" he cried, "ye shall no longer

11

bring disgrace and shame upon the honour of knight-hood. No longer shall ye march forth to rob and plunder. Know, thou leader of thy robber-troop, thy time is expired. Enter my hermitage, confess, and take the communion, for thou shalt never again ride living into the valley."

But the proud knight fell into a rage at the solemn admonition. "Punish the old bird of ill omen!" he cried in a fury, and rode away.

Now the hermitage chapel is wrapped in flames, and the aged hermit sinks to the ground from many wounds.

Dying, he stretches forth his hands in pain, and cries after the retreating knight, "Ride on, ride till the judgment day; ride every night through the forests, till thy horse sinks exhausted under thee, and may no pious one meet thee, but only the foul fiend of perdition!"

Mourning, the robber-band rode back to the high castle, for their leader had fallen with his horse and broken his neck.

They laid him in the still vault, but he cannot enjoy the peace of the grave. When the moonbeams fall soft and pale on castle and rocks, he tears in a wild gallop on his black horse below into the quiet valley.

To the grave of the hermit is the ghostly ride, and there, a grey, bleeding shadow, stands the murdered old man.

And a ghostly voice whispers, " Ride on, wicked knight, till the day of eternal retribution; but do not terrify the good—only the wicked. And where the stumbling of thy horse once brought thee death, there shall thy ride end—there shalt thou stumble every night."

Already long the castle has laid in ruins; but the knight rides ever, without rest, on a wild black steed from its lonely tower to the hermit's weeping-willow-shaded grave; and the enchantment can only be broken when the robber-knight, on his night ride, meets one more wicked than himself.

Legend of Silberhohl.

IN the neighbourhood of Leesen lies a spot called Silberhohl. It is almost round, and several feet deeper than the ground around it, and quite over-grown with swamp-moss. People go by with a shudder, for there is something the matter with the place.

Centuries ago a stately castle stood on the spot, in which there were always much drinking, gambling, and wild merriment.

The nobles of the castle acted as if they owned the whole world; and everything *did* belong to them that they could take by force, for they lived by robbing, and were guilty of much violence and cruelty.

One could say with truth, there was not a single good heart in the Burg except the young girl Jutta. Everybody loved her; and often, when the robbers had marched out to plunder, she would visit the poor and the sick, and even the robbed, giving them food and the money she had saved. The suffering and poor called her Saint Jutta.

Once the robbers had committed a monster crime. Covered with the blood of those they had robbed, they returned laden with booty to the castle.

Soon the goblets stood on the oaken tables, and the unholy, lawless revel began.

Suddenly the most terrible thunder rolled, a mighty flash of lightning swept the hall, the earth quaked and opened, the walls trembled, the tower shook and fell with an awful noise that was heard miles away. All sank in the gulf, which closed again, and nothing was left of the castle but a deep round spot where it had stood.

Many came to see the place so marked by a Divine vengeance, and every one said, " Poor Jutta !"

Not long after the destruction of the Burg, a poor woman in a neighbouring village fell ill. She wept sore, for her three little children cried for bread, and she could work no longer.

The mother folded her hands and prayed. Then she said to herself, " Oh! if the dear Jutta were only alive !"

Then the door was opened softly ; a light form

wrapped in a white veil, with a gleaming diadem in her hair, came forward to the bed.

" Jutta !" cried the poor mother.

The figure waved the hand, glanced kindly at the sleeping children, set down a peculiar shaped basket on a table, drew a cross over the mother, and vanished.

A deep sleep fell on the poor woman, and when she awoke the next morning she found the basket full of gold pieces.

Lautenthal. *

" *Harmonieen hör' ich klingen,*
Töne süsser Himmelsruh."

" Harmonies I hear resounding
Tones of sweet, heavenly music.

WHY dost thou sit so lonely on the declivity of the mountain, innocent daughter of the Felsenburg ? Why does the cloud of care rest on thy countenance ? Why dost thou gaze with such sad longing into the vale below ?

The light of thy eyes is dimmed by a tear ; heavy and anxious rests thy curly head on thy snowy arm. As the heavenly glory crowns the head of a martyred saint, so the splendour of sunset bathes thy form. Deep and great must be the anguish that fills thy breast, and yet thou dost endure speechless and silent. Not a sigh breaks from thy swelling heart,

* The valley of the lute.

not a lament from thy lips, not a sad note from the strings of the lute that lies hushed before thee.

Weep no longer, child of grief; brighten thy saddened countenance. He for whom thou art waiting—the beloved of thy soul—will come; he will come with the quick step of love, and his glance will chase away grief and care from thy soul.

Hark! Already it rustles in the wood, already his tread resounds on the rocks; he climbs the mountain.

With the bliss of the purest love he clasps the sorrowing maiden in his strong arms—and yet thou remainest in mourning and tears!

Fairest of the blue-eyed daughters of the Harz, is thy heart cold in presence of the flame of love, as the ice of the Brocken is proof against the sun of the spring-time?

Ah! not cold and hard was her heart. Pure and tender, as the dewdrops in the lily, it lay in her innocent breast, and adorned the morning of her life, till the sunny fire of love smiled down upon her. Then a never-before-imagined bliss trembled through the pure flower, her heart was filled with joy, the clear dewdrop dissolved in love. The dewdrop belongs to the sunbeams, and the heart of the maiden to the youth she loves.

But fate was not favourable to the lovers—fate, the destroyer of so many blissful bonds.

Jutta* was the daughter of a noble whose Schloss lay

* Pronounced Yootta.

near Leesen, and Ernst the son of an old warrior, who, after having fought many a battle in his youth and won many honours, now poor, weak from wounds, and forgotten by the world, had retired into solitude, to spend the remainder of his days in memories of his active life, and in the education of his only son. Under his guidance Ernst grew up strong and free, a true son of the Harz, lofty of stature and of an exalted mind, with a noble heart and countenance, with a fearless glance and bold design.

Where the Innerste, which springs from the Bärenbruche, approaches her issue from the Harz, she quickens her course, flowing among steep, well-wooded mountains in youthful mirth, or silently over sands, playing with the water-violets, which from the damp moss bend their blue heads in the crystal ripples. Beautiful rises on either bank the forest. Here grow mighty firs, whose roots spring from the metal-rich graywacke; there, slender beeches in the clay-slate; yonder, maples with their lovely leaves. Wild lettuce, yellow and red, grows next the round shave-grass, and the water-lily and mallow rock themselves on the fragrant banks; on the rocky mountain wall shimmers the white-browed swallow-wort, the saxifrage, and the yellow wall-pepper; from the mossy ground of the forest spring the flaming purple toad-stool, the agaric, and the pale goat's-beard.

The classic wood-singers fill the air with wondrous melodies.

From the topmost branches of the firs, where he has built his nest, the tiny greenfinch sings his little song. Beneath, on the river-banks, sounds the soft flute-like voice of the white-breasted plover, the whistling of the thistle-finch ; and the blackbird and linnet, the cross-bill and thrush make the green halls merry with their ringing voices.

In this valley, on the rushing, roaring Innerste, stood the cottage of unhewn trees and stones, covered with moss, in which father and son led a contented life. A small garden surrounded it, in which Ernst loved to work; there he listened to the tales of his father, or hunted in the mountain forests.

One day, as he had gone in the direction of Goslar, a singular howling fell upon his ear. He listened, recognized the howl of a wolf, mingled with the piercing neighing of a horse in deadly terror, and at the same time saw a rider tearing in fear over the mountains, without giving any heed to his calls.

He hurried in the direction of the neighing and howling, where he heard at the same time a female voice crying for help.

A large wolf hung on the neck of the almost prostrate horse, on whose back sat a charming maiden.

To see this, and with practiced hand to throw the javelin in the body of the beast of prey, that he sank at the feet of the horse, was the work of an instant. Quickly the youth thrust his hunting-knife in the beast, and the howlings ceased.

The maiden was saved, and looked gratefully upon her deliverer—and what a look! An unspeakable bliss penetrated his breast, he stood speechless before the pure rescued maiden, and his whole soul hung on her eye.

It was not the rosy cheek, not the crimson lips, that wounded his heart so deliciously, but her eye.

The horse was not able to carry her home, her servant had fled, and Ernst undertook to conduct her to her father's Burg. Arrived there, not all the entreaties of the rescued maiden could induce him to enter, but already it was difficult to tear himself away.

The impression she had made did not escape her notice, and as she gave him her hand at parting, carried away by the depth of her own emotions, she yielded to his entreaties to meet him sometimes, and promised with tears in her eyes.

Ernst hunted no more on the mountains, but stood dreaming on a high spot whence he could see her father's castle. And when he espied Jutta with her lute descend into the castle garden, and wander into the wood, he rushed to meet her, and lived a blissful hour in listening to her voice and lute, and she at last confessed she loved him with all her heart.

But now a rich earl sought Jutta's hand, and the lord of the Felsenburg promised this suitor his daughter, because his debts were so great that only a wealthy son-in-law could save his estates.

In vain Jutta threw herself at her father's feet and declared she loved a handsome, good, and noble youth of ancient race.

" Is he rich ? " was the father's sole question.

" No ! " Alas, " no ! " Ernst was in despair, and Jutta wept hours at a time, which only spoiled her pretty eyes without doing her the least good.

Jutta at last resolved to give up Ernst for her father's benefit, but she would see him once more, and assure him that her filial love could not lessen her affection for the choice of her heart.

That was what caused her sadness as we first saw her, and Ernst, as he rushed towards her, must have had some presentiment of the coming trouble in her resolve.   But she could not tell him her purpose, and, as they parted, whispered, " to-morrow we will see each other again."

The following day was nearly gone, and evening had sent on her shadow before her.   Jutta strengthened herself for her sad walk with a prayer, took her lute, and went through the garden into the forest, to the spot where she usually met her lover.

Ernst was not yet there.   She walked some distance in the direction of his cottage to a projection of the mountain, whence she could look down into the vale, and waited there for him.

Lost in her sad thoughts, her fingers swept lightly the strings of the lute, calling forth soft melodious notes.   Finding comfort in the tones, the harmonies grew louder and louder, and she listened with joy to the tones, now fancying them the voice of the nightingale or thrush.

At last her hands swept wildly over the strings in the strength of her sorrow.

Meanwhile Ernst had approached. He listened amazed to the tones, which floated to meet him, sounding entirely different from anything he had ever heard from Jutta's lute before.

It was as if a clear harmonious voice called back every note that flew from the strings.

Slowly and in indescribable purity the harmonies echoed through the mountains, and just where Ernst stood the sweet tones trembled in the air, as if the whole vale were one great harp.

"Can there be a cave here," thought Ernst, "which has such a wonderful echo?" and turned over a moss-grown stone with his foot. Who shall describe his astonishment as he saw a white shimmering stone before him, which extended so deep as he removed the moss?

His exclamation brought Jutta to his side, who at the sight threw herself into his arms with tears of joy.

"We are saved! It is silver!" they both exclaimed in the same breath.

Of course the earl received a *Korb*.* Ernst and

---

* *Korb*—basket. *Er hat einen Korb bekommen*, is the German "He has been rejected," "he has got the mitten;" that is, "he has got the basket."

Jutta were married. Ernst became the director of the mine, loaded with honours for his discovery, and ever since the valley has been called the Valley of the Lute.

Eva von Trotta.

A HISTORICAL TALE.

ON one of the border mountains, on the western slopes of the Harz, in gloomy desolation, rise the grey ruins of the old Schloss Staufenburg, which still remind us of a most romantic though sad history.

Home-like, and at the same time sublime, silent and solitary, must have been this now destroyed seat of Kaisers and princes in the mysterious Middle Ages. Its position is fascinating, surrounded on three sides by high wooded mountains with a wide view open to the south, which was then probably partially shut out by the primeval dense forests, now, however, extending over the little mining town of Gittelde and the picturesque mountain landscape to Osterode and the high-seated Schloss Herzberg.

The magic of this picture is greatly enhanced by the soft lights of sunset, and the dim, semi-transparent mists, which like a floating veil half hide its beauties, and fill the excited fancy with a mysterious presage of that poetic something we call the Past.

The mountain—on which are decaying bits of walls, where, until a few years ago, a strong square tower eighty feet in height, with openings here and there, looked solemnly down on the vale—is cut off sharp, on the east, west, and south sides from its wooded brethren that rise high above it, only on the north side sloping gradually to its base; and it is on this side one climbs to the spot where Kaiser Henry the Vogler, or Fowler, had a decoy for birds.

The halls trodden by royalty, the boudoirs where beauty ruled eight hundred years ago, are fallen into green ruin; the death-owl hoots, and bats and lizards house among their overgrown stones.

Many of these ruins on the borders of the Harz mountains remind us of Henry the Fowler, who built them to defend the plains and homes of this part of Germany from the wild and lawless Huns. As Duke of Saxony he is said to have lived here with his duchess, in this hunting-seat, when he was chosen Kaiser of the holy Roman Empire in 920; several other places, however, claim the honour.

Later the Staufenburg came to the Earls of Katlenburg, who had their seat near; and after the extinction of this house it fell into the hands of the mighty Duke Henry the Lion, of Saxony and Brunswick, before whose sword even the powerful Barbarossa trembled, and remained in the possession of his descendants, several of whom wore the imperial crown.

The Harz forests with their rich stores of game attracted not seldom the hunt-loving princes of Brunswick to their deep shades, and horn and hound and the wild ho ho ! hio hi! of the hunter were heard over mountain and vale.

Then came a calmer period for the old Staufenburg, as the retired seat of princely widows, and here lived, in the fourteenth century, the Duchess Elizabeth, widow of William the Younger.

Oblivion at last sits green a couple of centuries in this solitude, till it is chosen as the hiding-place of a sinful love, and wild tales came to be told among the simple mountaineers of a White Lady who haunted the castle.

On the grey stone balcony stood, one summer day in 1537, two persons in close conversation.

The lady, arrayed in white, was of remarkable and striking beauty. A tall form of the most perfect symmetry, brilliant white complexion, cheeks of a delicate rose, very large clear blue eyes, dark brown hair falling in luxuriant natural curls, and a dainty hand and foot, made her the delight of every eye that looked upon her.

The grace of all her movements seemed akin to poetry and music, and the expression of her radiant countenance betokened a noble and amiable mind.

Her companion, Duke Henry the Younger, of Brunswick-Lüneburg-Wolfenbüttel, clasped one of her tiny hands glittering with diamonds, in his own, stroked her magnificent hair, and gazed into her face with silent rapture.

It was nearly five o'clock in the afternoon, and the

coffee table, according to German custom at this hour stood in the garden below draped in white, a silver coffee service glittered on the table, fragrant mountain strawberries lent a rich bit of colouring, and by one cup lay a spray of white roses.

The broken fountain suggested a feeling of loneliness, and the high old grey stone walls enclosing the castle shut it out—or in—from the world beyond, and all the events now transpiring behind them were a profound secret. The white robed figure was literally dead and buried to the world, which had "assisted" at her funeral.

"Oh, Henry!" exclaimed Eva von Trotta, for the youthful form belongs to no other than this Fair Rosamond of Germany, "you strive to comfort me, but in vain. All your words of kindness and passionate love, cannot crush the worm that is gnawing at the thread of my life—cannot silence the voice of conscience. I must open my heart to you to-day, for every visit you make me here I tremble to think may be the last. And yet it is all wrong—all wrong, Henry; every visit, every gift from your dear hand is a sin against the good and noble-minded Duchess, once my motherly friend, a sin against your lawful children."

"Dear Eva," said Henry, interrupting her, "*our* children are lawful. I gave you my left hand at the altar, the wedding-ring and its diamond keeper glitter on this little hand I hold in mine. The Church has consecrated our union."

"That is only a hollow pretence. I see it all now.
Look at this beautiful Prayer Book in gold and precious stones, and the Bible* with my name in gold on
its cover," she continued, pointing to a small table
where they lay.

"They were among your gifts on our—our—our
marriage day. I come and sit here when alone,
where I can look out on the mountains, and read
them and seek consolation, but find none. They
are a silent reproach to me. You had no right
to give them, nor I to take them. And in my Bible
I opened yesterday to St. Paul's words: '*the husband
of one wife.*' They pierced like daggers to my heart.
Henry, Henry, I ought to flee this spot, and never see
you more; and yet I cannot. I should die if I did not
see your dear face sometimes, and hear your.

"My darling Eva, put away these harrowing
thoughts; they are shortening your precious life."

"Oh! why did we meet? or meeting, why was it
not earlier, when our love had been no sin? When
I recall the affection and confidence of the Duchess,
and reflect on my base, false friendship, my face
burns with pain and shame. The world would curse
me; she would too, if she knew. The watch I wear,
that you gave me that last morning in the antechamber when I was on duty as lady-in-waiting, reminds me of the flight of time, and the unceasing

* Luther's Bible appeared two years before this scene. Eva was
Protestant.

approach of a coming judgment. I never look upon it without a throb of bitter anguish. 'Nothing that loveth or maketh a lie' shall enter heaven—*and my life is a lie.* Oh, Henry! I shall perish eternally, and my noble boy will grow up to curse my memory;" and leaning her head on Henry's breast, she wept bitterly.

Probably Henry's own reflections were not of the most agreeable and consoling character, as he was thus compelled to recall his injustice and sin in his neglect of the Duchess. He gave, however, no expression to his misgivings, but only said pointing to the coffee-table: "Let us think of this no more; dry up these childish tears, and let us go down—come, dear."

"My tears are not childish, Henry, only useless. But the world will discover our dreadful secret, the Duchess and her powerful father will complain to Kaiser and Pope, your visits will be forbidden—and what will become of me and my boy?"

"Eva, I will do what I before proposed, before you came here. I will seek a divorce from the Duchess, and we will be married in the face of the empire, and your boy, my favourite son, shall be my heir to the ducal throne."

"God forbid!" cried Eva in feverish, wild excitement, clasping her hands and looking up to heaven, in which attitude she presented such an enchanting grace and beauty that Henry caught her in his arms

12

and covered her face and hair with kisses, calling her by every endearing name he could think of.

" No, Henry ; never, never will I be guilty of such a gigantic wrong. My son shall never be your heir, shall never supplant your first-born son and lawful heir. My noble Eitel* is noble in character as in name ; he would never consent, no more than I. But I live in constant terror of discovery."

" Do not fear that, my darling ; every servant here is bound by a solemn oath ; your faithful nurse Magda is the only one who is permitted to leave the castle, and she does so in the deepest disguise. The priest at Gandersheim who united us at the convent altar is bound by his priestly vows, and the heavy bribe I gave him, to silence. The Abbess, too, who managed the details of your funeral, and the artistic priest who made your wax effigy and the plague-spots with ink on your white face and hands, are both bound by the most solemn oaths. None of these will ever betray us, and no one else knows our secret—we are safe.

Henry was right. Though this relation continued seven years, and ended only through Eva's death, no one discovered the secret ; he himself revealed it in his partial love for her only son, whom he sought to make his heir. But the lovers little imagined that one person knew Eva was not lying in the damp vaults of the convent, and that they would be at the mercy of this discoverer.

* *Eitel*—Noble.

Their conversation was interrupted by the entrance of the little Eitel Henry, a princely boy, who inherited his mother's striking beauty, his long brown curls falling over his shoulders.

"Come, *Mütterchen*,* coffee is ready, and I have put some white roses for you, and Babette has brought mountain strawberries ; come—come, Papa," and the little fellow put up his mouth for a kiss. The mother stooped and covered his head and face with passionate kisses, and Henry, springing forward, enclosed them both in a tender embrace.

Behind came nurse Gretchen in snowy cap and apron, with a lovely babe in her arms, and both parents sprang forward as if each would be the first to seize the child.

To a stranger who had not been behind the scenes it was an innocent and pure family scene, betraying nothing of the wrong and bitterness these relations had caused. To explain further, we must go back in our history to Eva's childhood, and her introduction to the court of Henry the Younger, Duke of Brunswick, and his Duchess Maria von Würtemberg.

A lovely spring morning dawned joyously over the castle of the Marshal Adam von Trotta—or Troth—of Brandenburg, but sorrow housed within it, for the lady of the castle must die. The invalid reclined on a huge old-fashioned sofa, propped up with silken cushions, surrounded by her husband, her two sons, and her

---

* *Little mother*—a term of endearment expressed by the diminutive, which form is frequently employed in the German language.

young and only daughter Eva. It was a large and richly-furnished chamber, hung with rare paintings, but the most charming pictures of all were the views its windows commanded.

The dying mother kissed and dismissed her children, knowing it was for the last time. The manly youths kissed the mother's emaciated hand and silently retired, but Eva flung herself sobbing on her breast, and refused to be comforted.

At last the Marshal led her from the room.

"We are alone for the last time," said the invalid, as the Marshal returned, putting her hand in his. "Move me nearer the window, that I may look once more on the park I love so well."

After a pause she exclaimed, " My poor motherless Eva!—as she will be before this morning's sun goes down. I can leave my sons with more resignation, for they are noble youths, and able to fight the world's battles ; but Eva has the dangerous gift of an unusual beauty, and the world is full of snares and traps for such as she promises to be."

"She is your image when I brought you home a young wife.* She has your eyes, your brown curls, now touched with grey, and to me dearer than ever. In her I shall see your form and face every hour."

"Nurse Magda has promised me never to leave her,

---

* In Germany one never says *Braut*—bride—after the marriage ; but *die junge Frau*—young wife. *Braut* is employed during the engagement.

and her foster-sister Alice, who is strongly attached to her, will be of great assistance in watching over her as they both grow older. Keep Eva with you as long as you can, but in the event of a campaign send her to your brother."

The speaker, exhausted, sank into a peaceful slumber, and when the setting sun illuminated the chamber, its golden beams fell upon the face of death.

They laid the mother in the old family vault; husband and children brought immortelles and roses for her coffin, and left her to her cold but safe repose.

The Marshal did as his dying wife had counselled, and kept Eva in the parental castle till her sixteenth summer. The bud had blossomed into a wonderful flower, the pride of the desolate father's heart.

But the time has arrived when the soldier must go forth to battle, and Eva is sent to her aunt and uncle for a visit of indefinite length. At this period, undecided as to Eva's home, and depressed with fears and anxieties regarding her future, business calls the Marshal to the Court of Brunswick,* then held in the ancient Castle of Wolfenbüttel,† and this visit is destined to decide the fate of the youthful Eva.

The piety and amiability of the Duchess Maria made such a deep impression on the mind of the statesman and soldier, that he entreated her to become the guardian of his motherless daughter. Her Trans-

* *Bruno's Wyck*—Bruno's settlement, or town.
† *Wolfenbüttel*—wolf's cave.

parency consented, and Eva became first lady-in-waiting to the Duchess.

Little did the father imagine he was thrusting his child into the wolf's den, for a worse example of a false and neglectful husband than Henry the Younger of Brunswick-Wolfenbüttel it were not easy to find.

The Duke and Duchess were in no wise congenial spirits. Henry was a handsome man of fiery temper and hot blood, loved both chase and feud, possessed more physical strength and beauty than mind or virtue, troubled himself little with the duties of government or the interests of his subjects, leaving affairs of State to his minister.

Henry had no sympathy for prayers and church-going, neglected his pale, youthful wife, seldom visiting the wing of the gloomy old castle she occupied except when etiquette demanded his presence.

In this deplorable state of things Eva von Trotta appeared at Court. She stood in the courtyard by her father's war-horse to take leave of him, promised to be good, which promise she fully intended to keep; the stern old soldier kissed her, sprang on his horse, brushed away a tear which defied all his iron firmness, stormed over the drawbridge, and never saw his fair child again.

Suddenly it began to be reported at Court that Henry had bridged over the cleft between himself and his high-born wife. He was seen every evening at her side in the stone balcony, whence they could look down

into the courtyard and witness the sports of the
courtiers and the drilling of steeds, and his conjugal
attentions were most edifying to witness; while the
new maid of honour, Eva, stood behind the seat of
her ducal mistress, a picture of bewildering love-
liness.

But the Court did not permit itself long to be deceived by the royal hypocrite. It was not the pale,
pious Duchess who had so suddenly fascinated Henry,
but the maid of honour, radiant in black Genoa velvet
and silver spangles, into whose clear blue eyes Henry's
brown ones looked so willingly.

It soon became perfectly well known to Henry
when Eva was on duty in the antechamber of the
Duchess, and half-hidden by the heavy hangings of the
deep windows, he chatted with her by the hour, and
no favourite maid dared tell her royal mistress who
entertained the lady-in-waiting while she sat alone.

At last, one day, the Mistress of the Robes, who had
more than once reproved Eva for frivolity, and whose
curiosity had got the better of her dignity, listens and
hears Henry ask Eva to meet him in the evening at
ten o'clock in the linden allée for a walk to the arbour
at the end of it, and the thoughtless girl consents. At
the same time she sees Henry present her with a watch
and his portrait.

Horrified, she at once informs the Duchess of this
proposed rendezvous, and persuades her to accompany
her in disguise to the arbour at the appointed hour,

where, concealed behind the thick foliage, she might learn what was best to be done.

Later on this same day Eva sat alone in her boudoir gazing at the portrait, an exquisite enamel set in diamonds. It was a beautiful chamber, adorned with frescoes and paintings, mirrors, panellings, books and flowers.

Opposite where Eva was sitting hung a life-size portrait of Duke Henry the Lion in tapestry. The old nurse, Magda, had just left her beloved young mistress, and Eva held the portrait in her hand, while a tumult of emotions shook her heart.

She was interrupted by a knock, and slipped the portrait hastily out of sight. It was her foster-sister Alice, who was her favourite maid.

"Why do you disturb me at this hour, Alice?" inquired her mistress, who struggled to conceal her emotion. "You know I am in the habit of spending this hour alone."

"Pardon, gracious lady, but I have something to tell you which admits of no delay," replied Alice, who had caught a glimpse of the portrait, and noticed the agitation of her mistress. "I wish to leave the Court. It is my wish to enter the convent of Gandersheim. I intend to become a nun."

"Become a nun! When did that insane idea enter your head?"

"I am weary of the Court. I am unhappy here. Let me go."

Alice did not tell her of the Court gossip she had overheard, and that grief and pain drove her to the convent.

"Magda will not leave me, Alice; why will you? Stay with me. You knew my dear mamma; you are nearly of my own age; I should miss you sadly."

"No, I have determined to take the veil; it is my calling. Let me go."

Eva sighed, and replied, rising and laying her hand on Alice's shoulder, at the same time glancing nervously at the portrait of Henry the Lion, "I am not happy either, dear Alice. Oh! I wish I had never left my uncle's castle, and the protection of my brothers. Why was I doomed to lose my mother? You seem to me more like a friend than a servant, Alice; how can I do without you, my foster-sister?"

Again Eva paused and listened. Suddenly the portrait of Henry the Lion advanced into the room, and Duke Henry stood in the opening it had left in the wall. Eva flushed, turned pale, and stood in confusion, while Alice looked on in bewildered amazement. But Henry said carelessly, "The Duchess is coming, Fräulein von Trotta; I am only a minute in advance."

Alice saluted and retired, muttering to herself, "It is true, then, and worse than I thought. A secret door. And what does that portrait mean? I wonder if mother knows all this."

The following day Alice departed for the convent.

The castle clock was ringing ten when two muffled figures stole through a postern gate of the garden wall behind it into the park, and, concealed by the darkness, hastened through by-paths to the lime-tree arbour. Here they waited some time, when at last steps and voices were heard approaching through the lime-tree avenue.

Eva was saying, " Do not ask me to stay at Court, Henry. I cannot, I must go at once. The courtiers are talking ; Alice insists on leaving me. I know it is out of sorrow she condemns me who am so far innocent. Think of my youth—I am only sixteen. My mother is dead, my father absent. Oh, I cannot deceive the Duchess. She has been so kind to me, and she is so good. I shall return your presents, which I should never have accepted, and go back to my uncle's little castle."

" And forsake me, and leave me to loneliness and wretchedness ? Oh, Eva ! pity me and remain."

" And bring disgrace and misery and ruin upon you and myself, and anguish to the Duchess ? Maria's royal father is all-powerful with the Kaiser, who would betray you to the Pope, and you would be excommunicated. I do love you, Henry—but—it is too late. If we had met earlier we might have belonged to each other. I would live shut out from the world for ever for you, and you alone, and, safe from disturbance and discovery, would be happy."

" How very noble and self-sacrificing we would be !"

exclaimed the Duchess, coming forward from her concealment. "And such is my reward for my affection
bestowed upon a motherless maiden ! To such a shame-
ful conversation must I listen between her and my
husband. But I have the power to punish you both,
and I will use it ; " and the Duchess and her attendant
speedily disappeared in the darkness.

The storm had broken upon them. The two figures
stood in the arbour, motionless as marble, while Maria
hastened to send messengers immediately to her father
and other princes, acquainting them of Henry's perfidy.

But Eva at bay seems suddenly to have changed
her character. She forgets her former scruples, and
with a single move checkmates her rival, but at what
a cost ! She proposes perhaps the most extraordinary
plan that ever entered a human brain, and all the more
astounding as coming from a girl of sixteen.

"What is to become of me ?" at last exclaimed Eva,
starting from the stupor of terror the sudden appearance of the Duchess had caused. "There is not a
place where I can go where disgrace and shame will
not follow me."

" I will seek a divorce, declare the children of the
Duchess illegitimate, and we will be married."

"Under the ban of Kaiser and Pope !" cried Eva,
wringing her hands in despair.

After a pause, in which Eva remained buried in
thought, she resumed, " I have a plan, Henry, but the
world shall know nothing of our secret. You shall

give me your left hand, but I *must die*—I mean *seem*
to.   I shall resign my office at Court and retire, osten-
sibly to return to my uncle's.   On the journey I will
be attacked with the plague in the convent of Gandersheim, and die in a few hours ; and then there must be a
public funeral ; the world and the Court shall see me
buried.   I leave the carrying out of the details to you.
Leave Wolfenbüttel on some plausible plea, and in
your absence I will retire.   Dead to the world, I will
live only for you."

Henry, enraptured, caught her in his arms.

"My darling Eva! will you indeed do that! Oh!
then I am happy, and could defy the world.   Here is
the seal of our bond," and he placed a diamond ring on
her finger.

They walked arm-in-arm under the silent lindens
back to the castle.   The moon had risen, and bathed
the night in her mystic light ; the stars looked mournfully down on the betrayed maiden.   Was there no
hand to save her from this ruinous step—no voice to
warn the betrayer of his sin ?

The following day, after a stormy scene between
the Duke and Duchess, Henry left the castle to attend
to business, as he said, and on his return found that
the new maid of honour had resigned her office and
left the Court.

The Capuchin convent of Gandersheim, situated in
the Duchy of Brunswick, on the river Gande, enjoyed

an equal rank with the abbeys of Drübeck and Quedlinburg. The Abbesses of these three mitred convents*
had a seat and vote in the Reichstag, and during the
earliest period of their existence the Abbesses were of
the blood-royal, and only princesses and daughters of
the nobility were admitted into their sacred retirement.

This imperial convent Gandersheim, once endowed
with such wealth and power, was founded by Duke
Ludolf of Saxony in the last half of the ninth century.
It obtained its greatest power under the Ottos, and the
imperial princesses were often sent here for their education, or for security in times of danger. To this ancient
convent I must beg my readers to accompany me.

It is midnight. A fearful tempest sweeps over the
mountains. The *Wilde Jäger*† is out with his ghostly
train, and *Tut-Ursel's*‡ howlings ring through the
darkness.

The rain beats against the windows of the convent
as if it would force an entrance, flashes of lightning
illuminate the night, and the thunder shakes the old
building in its fury, as if it would uproot its very
foundations.

Before a convent altar stands a bridal pair. The
bridegroom places the nuptial ring on the bride's hand ;
kneeling they receive the priest's blessing, the young

---

* *Mitred convents*—those which had a right to a seat and vote in
the Reichstag. . † Wild Hunter.

‡ *Tut Ursel*—Tooting Ursula—the nun who broke her vow.

wife rises Frau von Kirchberg, and after remaining some days in concealment in the convent, she escapes in the disguise of a monk to Schloss Staufenburg.

Meanwhile tidings reach the Court at Wolfenbüttel that the retired Court lady has been attacked with a virulent plague on her homeward journey, and has expired after a painful illness of only a few hours.

The Court is aghast at the news; Henry retires to his private apartments. Duchess Maria, softened to hear of the lady Eva's death, sends members of her Court to attend the funeral.

And now we have the second act of the drama in old Gandersheim.

The convent church is brilliant with a thousand tapers. High on a rich catafalque before the great altar stands Eva's coffin in a blaze of light. The face of the dead is of a wondrous beauty, the long brown curls fall over the breast, the small white hands, marked with plague-spots, are crossed above the still, cold heart.

The nuns, the Abbess at their head, chant the mournful dirge, and the organ weeps and wails as if it were the very soul of sorrow. The courtiers wear the deepest black, and are completely overwhelmed with the awful solemnity of the scene.

Through all the ceremony the novice Alice seems like one in a dream. The suddenness of the thing is to her incomprehensible. Only a few days ago she took leave of her foster-sister, and now she gazes on the dead! Finally the coffin is lowered; they are about to close it for ever, when Alice, before the Abbess or the two priests, who alone knew the truth, can prevent her, rushes forward with a cry of agony and kisses the cold hands in her sorrow. Suddenly she discovers they are only wax! Conscious of the danger to herself if she betrays her discovery, she weeps and sobs louder than ever, and must be almost forcibly removed. They bear the coffin to the convent vaults, the courtiers return to the Court to picture the marvellous beauty of the departed Eva to the Duke and Duchess.

In the meantime the novice Alice is no novice. She ponders over the matter in secret.

" Eva is not dead," she reflects. "Where can she be? What can it all mean ? I will find her if I walk every inch of the Harz mountains. I will disguise myself as an old woman, a seller of lace ; thus I can gain admittance everywhere. But I must get away from here without exciting suspicion."

As the result of these soliloquies, Alice informs the Abbess she must relinquish her plan of becoming a nun, at least for the present, and go to her mother, who must be in great distress at the sudden loss of her nursling.

But on her arrival at the castle of Wolfenbüttel, Magda has disappeared, and no one knows what has become of her.

For a period of four years, Alice, disguised in a

grey wig, with an artificial hump on her back, sought Eva, wandering from castle to castle, from town to town through the mountains; but without discovering the faintest trace of Eva or nurse Magda.

The princes of the House of Brunswick were, as I said before, passionate lovers of the chase, and Henry the Younger was no exception to his race. But suddenly this *penchant* increased to such an extent that his time was almost entirely absorbed with this pastime.

He began to be absent weeks and even months in his favourite Harz.

At length these long absences excited the suspicions of the Court and the Duchess. Tales came to their ears of a lady in white, who had been seen at the deserted old Staufenburg. Spies were sent out several times to watch the castle, but no discovery was made. Eva remained dead to the world.

Alice, who heard these reports, knowing what others did not, that Eva was not in the vaults of the convent at Gandersheim, resolved to make a visit to the Staufenburg, thinking it very likely the reports of the lady in white were not simply wild mountain tales, but having some truth in them. This she felt to be all the more probable, since in all her ramblings from town to castle no trace of the lost girl was to be found.

Accordingly Alice made her way to the Staufenburg, and after watching from the thick woods three whole days she saw her mother, Magda, issue from a small postern door in the outer walls, so hidden by trees and underbrush as to be unseen when shut.

Alice hastened to meet her, secure of her disguise, and told her she had a special message from the Master to the Lady Eva, and must speak with her alone.

Magda, terrified, exclaimed, " Who are you ? Whom do you mean by the Lady Eva ?"

"I am one who knows all the secret, and that the beautiful maid of honour, Eva von Trotta, does not lie in her coffin. Better if she did. But my message is pressing and admits of no delay. My orders are to deliver it to the lady alone. Admit me here, and leave the door unlocked that I may let myself out again."

Magda stared at the old hump-backed woman and her basket and hesitated ; but seeing she knew the secret, at last concluded all was right.

"Follow me," she said ; and opening the postern door and pointing out to her an outer flight of stone steps leading down to a garden, continued, "mount those steps leading to the stone balcony. You will find the lady you seek in her boudoir, which you enter from that open door. She is alone. I will wait for you here, for I dare not leave the gate open. It might be discovered, for I have seen people prowling about here lately a good deal."

Alice did as directed. Arrived on the balcony she paused and gazed at the graceful but passive figure

13

half reclining in a fauteuil in full view of the mountains.

Eva is now in her twenty-first year, and lovelier than ever. Her face and hands are so white as to seem almost transparent; her curls fall in rich masses over her white silken robe; her blue eyes have a strange far-away look in them that strikes Alice to the heart.

Suddenly Eva becomes aware of the presence of a stranger, starts out of her pensive reverie and exclaims, " Who are you ? How did you get in the garden ?"

" I met a servant at the postern gate in the wall," replied Alice in a constrained voice. " I told her I had a special message for you."

" From Henry ? Then you know all ! Quick ! quick ! What is it ?

Alice hesitated, for she was so moved at sight of her playmate and foster-sister, she could not command her voice to speak.

" Why are you so long ? Speak. I will reward you richly if you bring me good news from Duke Henry."

" I do not bring you a message from Henry of Brunswick, but from God," said Alice, slowly and solemnly. " Leave this castle, forget Henry, return to the path of duty and virtue, and seek forgiveness."

" Who are you ?" cried the terrified Eva, springing from her seat. " If the Duke did not send you, who did ? Oh ! I am betrayed ! Magda ! Magda ! What have you done ?"

"Do not fear, White Lady of the Staufenburg, I will not betray you. I have sought you four long years, because I love you, and would save you from a life-long wretchedness. I was at your imagined funeral, and discovered the farce, but no mortal save myself knows of my discovery.

"Who are you? Why do you come here? to threaten, to torment me? Do you want money?"

"Why do I come? You are in danger. The Duchess has spies; stories of a White Lady in the Staufenburg are come even to the Court. The Duke's long absences excite suspicion. He is watched. Think of the storm that will burst upon you both if you are discovered. Leave here before it is too late."

"Why do you interest yourself for a lonely creature like me, dead and buried?"

"You do not know me—how could you? My own mother did not recognize me," and Alice threw off hump and wig, and stood before Eva, a tall, well-formed girl, nearly her own age.

"Alice!" cried Eva, rushing to her, and seizing her in her arms. "I thought you were a nun in the convent of Gandersheim. You are come to stay with me. Oh! say you are come to stay."

"No, I will not stay here. I have sought you all this time as an old lace-seller, to warn and save you. If you will give up Henry and leave this den of sin, I will follow you wherever you go. Oh! what words

can I use to induce you to leave here? Eva! Eva!
it is your foster-sister, your truest friend, who entreats
you. Henry is your worst enemy. He has trodden
your honour and name in the dust, but you consented,
and destroyed what you might have been for ever.
But repentance is left, and there is all eternity to
come.

"How can you stand before God? how can you dare
pray? You desecrated the holiest; virtue and innocence you have made the tools of vice; you have stolen
the *monstrance* from the altar; you swore a false oath
before the altar of the Highest. Talk of a left-handed
marriage. It is an insult to Heaven's laws. Eva!
Eva! once my pure and dear playmate, the darling of
your dead mother's heart, come away with me now—
now. No one is here to betray our flight. We will
go to some distant land, and I will stay with you so
long as we both live. Follow your true friend. It is
the voice of Heaven you hear. Forget the unworthy
murderer of your youth and purity."

Eva trembled and turned pale. "What would become of my children?" she cried, wringing her hands
in anguish.

"Children! have you children?"

"Yes, three. See, that is my noble Eitel with the
long brown curls, playing in the garden."

"God will protect them. You can do nothing for
them even if you remain. They are in the power of
their father. Come, come; oh, listen to the voice of

warning before it is too late," and Alice seized Eva's hand as if she would lead her away.

"I cannot! I cannot! I love Henry. Love his princely magnanimity, his bravery, his noble pride— even that which others hate in him I love. For him I have robbed the Duchess of her husband, deceived my brave father and my brothers, desecrated God's altar, sacrificed life, youth, honour, happiness; I live only for him. I cannot deceive him, cannot atone for one sin with another."

"I must save you, then, by telling your brothers where you are. They will punish the vile Henry before the whole German Empire." She released Eva's hand and turned to go.

With a scream Eva sprang forward, threw herself down before Alice, clasped her knees and cried, "Be merciful, Alice; have pity on my misery. God is merciful. Do not you be cruel. Do not betray me. I am crushed and bruised, the peace of my mind and heart destroyed. I could not be more wretched. What good would it do to betray me? and in betraying Henry, you destroy me, rob me of the only earthly protection I can ever hope to enjoy. Magda is a mother to my children as she was to me. She would not betray me.

"My mother was your nurse, hence has a mother's feelings for you. I will not stay here. If I should see Henry, I should forget all respect for his person as Duke, and give him a piece of my mind. I will keep your secret, but I warn you of a coming danger. Then I can be of more service to you without than if I stayed here. God help you. I will not betray you." And hastily assuming her disguise, for footsteps were heard approaching, she hurried away.

Three years passed away after this interview, and Eva remained securely hidden; but Henry's absences from Court grew longer and more frequent, and at last one of the courtiers resolved to penetrate the mystery.

He followed Henry to the Staufenburg, watched four whole days in the thick woods, and the evening of the fourth day, to his utter amazement, recognized Eva von Trotta in the stone balcony by Henry's side. The secret was out! He hastened to the Duchess and told her what he had seen. Maria sent authorized messengers to the convent of Gandersheim, the coffin bearing Eva's name was broken open, and lo! a wooden figure with wax mask and hands!

The Duchess communicates this discovery to the King of Würtemburg, her father, letters of reproof are sent to Henry from him and the Kaiser, and the Pope threatens him with excommunication.

Henry hastens to Eva with the dreadful news; but Alice has been before him, and Eva is prepared with another plan.

" Tell them to search the Staufenburg, and they will discover their mistake. Tell them I am dead—it is true. Magda shall conduct the children to Kirchberg, and with Alice's aid they and every trace of my having been here will vanish. I have a secure hiding-place."

" Where, Eva ?"

" You shall know to-morrow on your return from Gandersheim, Henry."

She took an affectionate and reluctant leave of him, calling him back two or three times before she could let him go.

Then she sent for her children, wept over them, and gave her directions to Magda and Alice, and cut off Eitel's long curls that he might not be recognized, his resemblance to her with his long hair being so striking.

After she had dismissed them, Eva returned to her boudoir and wrote a note to Henry. Then she took a small flask from her writing-table, poured its contents in a glass of water, and reclining in her fauteuil, drank it.

Henry, on his return the following morning, hastened to Eva's boudoir.

Seeing Eva seated, and not springing up as usual to welcome him, he supposed she had fallen asleep— and so she had ; but a sight of her face revealed the dreadful truth. She had taken poison. The empty flask lay on the writing-table beside her ; near it a note addressed to himself. He tore it open. It only contained a few words.

" I told you, my beloved Henry, I had a secure

hiding-place. I meant the grave. Tell them I am
dead. They cannot follow where I am going. I
would not bring ruin on you and your dominions.
Oh, Henry! be good to my children, and never
attempt to make Eitel your heir. My sin was loving
you. Farewell.

" Yours in death, Eva."

Duke Henry had the broken-hearted girl—only
twenty-three—buried in the garden of the Staufenburg, returned to Court and insisted on a search of
the castle. They did search, of course discovering
nothing, and the mystery was still impenetrable.

The Duchess Maria died a few months after her
rival, and nothing was ever known of the well-guarded
secret, until Henry himself betrayed it in his partiality
for his favourite son Eitel Henry—Eva's only son and
eldest child. The Duke besought the Pope to recognize him as the heir to the ducal throne, offering a
heavy bribe. His Holiness consented, the more
readily since the Duke's lawful heir, Henry Julius, had
become a Protestant.

But Eitel proved himself, as his mother had said,
noble in character as in name. He absolutely refused
his consent to this injustice, and lived in retirement on
the estate Kirchberg, which the Duke had given him,
the name of which Eva's children bore. The Kirch-
bergs, however, soon became extinct.

The learned Duke Henry Julius, founder of a

university, never forgot the refusal of his noble illegitimate brother to deprive him of his birthright, and ever remained his warm friend.

There were two castles in the Harz mountains, both of which bore the name of Staufenburg; that near Zorge, an hour and a half from the beautiful ruins of Convent Walkenried. It is said to have been occupied during the Thirty Years' War. When built or by whom destroyed are matters of conjecture. The Staufenburg of our tale is near Gittelde. Some derive the name from the idol *Stuvo*, or *Stuffo*, once set up on the mountain. The mountain was so steep that *Staufen*, or *Stufen*—steps—were used in climbing it, hence probably the name.

The Weingarten Höhle and the Three Men.

THERE is perhaps no cave in all Germany concerning which so many legends and traditions are in the mouth of the people as this Weingartenloch.

A plank crosses over a black piece of water from the outer portion of the cave farther into the darkness, far from human help and human voices.

The tradition is, that whoever crosses that beam will be given over to the Evil One, who governs there, and sits, between heaps of gold and silver, by a table, with a great book before him, in which he writes the name of every person who approaches him.

But when three enter together, and draw lots with one another, two of them may depart laden with treasures, and only the third, upon whom the lot has fallen, must remain behind, and is torn in a thousand pieces by the demon.

Two men from some distant country had often entered the cave, and had always succeeded in enticing a third to accompany them, who always fell into the hands of the *Gott-sei-bei-uns*, since they arranged it that the lot fell to him.

Finally, it struck the inhabitants as something very remarkable that those who had entered the cave with the two strangers never returned, and henceforth they failed to find a follower.

Then they entered the hut of a poor man in Dorf Osterhagen, who had a wife and eight children, and challenged him with brilliant promises to follow them into the cave.

The man, whose name was Schlosser, felt little inclination for the expedition, and absolutely refused, even if they offered him eighty Thaler.

But the wife called her husband into another room, and said to him: " Thou knowest that I love thee dearly, and would sink from sorrow and anguish if thou shouldst be torn from me ; but we have eight children, and no bread in the cupboard, and no money, and with the money the strangers offer thee we should have enough for our whole lives ; so go with them, and be sure no evil will befall thee."

And she opened a cupboard, took out a plant, sewed it in his shirt in three different places, made a sign of the cross above each place, and said, "That which I have sewed in thy shirt is *origanum*, a sure defence against all enchantment, and even the devil ; so go in peace, in the name of the Father, and the Son, and the Holy Ghost. Amen."

And Schlosser embraced his wife and children, and went with the two men, who looked, scornfully laughing, at each other, after having laid eighty glittering new Thaler on the table.

They wandered on until they had reached the beam —the fatal beam—where they stood still, and the men warned Schlosser solemnly, if his life was dear to him, to utter no sound till they had passed the next two caves.

Schlosser promised, and the three crossed cautiously the dangerous bridge, and entered a cave filled with the most horrible vermin.

Bombinas and salamanders seemed to be giving a ball. Bats fluttered thick as a hailstorm through the air. Terrible serpents and dragons coiled hissing around each other, The most hideous brood of nature was flocked together, and swarmed around the feet of the three men entering, as if to form a wall to hinder their entrance.

With firmness the three went directly forward toward a second cave, which was large and lofty, and lighted with a magical splendour.

At the right, against the rocky wall, shimmering

with gold and silver, stood a couch of red velvet embroidered in gold, and on the silken cushions lay a sleeping maiden of such super-terrestrial beauty, that Schlosser could not take his eyes from the picture, and was drawn forward by force by his companions. In the next cave they stood still, drew a long breath, looked anxiously at each other, and put down their lamps.

" Now, dear friend," said one of the men to Schlosser, " the moment is come. In a quarter of an hour we may become rich and happy, or for ever lost in perdition. Immeasurable wealth is in the cave we are about to enter, but only two of us can become possessed of the accumulated treasures, or ever see the light of day again ; the third, on whom the lot falls, must remain as a sacrifice to the dark ruler of the subterranean world. Be firm and follow us !"

Schlosser felt as if paralysed by lightning at the terrible disclosure, and without knowing what he did, he followed the two, who went on before, and knocked three times on a small iron door.

Cracking, it sprang open, and a blood-red splendour shone forth in the great space which they now entered. Gold, silver, and precious stones lay in colossal heaps on every side, and the place sparkled and shone so, that even the anxious Schlosser's heart was filled with joy.

But now from a corner a man of lofty stature came forward, with sparkling, burning eyes, black, bristly hair, dark, bushy eyebrows, and a crooked, arched hawk-nose.

In a frightful, peculiar manner he twitched his yellow face; and his garments were strange and odd. A fiery-red gold-bordered mantle hung in bunchy folds from his shoulders; a broad, drooping Spanish hat, with a long, waving red plume, sat sideways on his head, and a long rapier hung at his side.

With a slight bow he passed the three men, and vanished through the iron door, by which they had entered.

The two men now challenged Schlosser to help them fill their sacks, and as soon as that was done they returned through the iron door, which shut with a loud crash behind them.

"I cannot tell how it is with me to-day," said one stranger to his friend. "I am filled with fear, and my teeth chatter, and it creeps like fire in my veins. If only some misfortune does not meet us!"

"Thou art very foolish," replied the other. "Is it not the eighteenth time that we have been here, and we have always known how to turn and shuffle that the lot fell on the accompanying third person? And where could we have found a better companion than that fellow there, out of whose eyes the most charming simplicity and stupidity look, so that a child might deceive him?"

He would have added more, but Schlosser, who went on before, uttered a cry of horror, and the hearts of the two friends sank within them, although what they saw they had seen already eighteen times.

On the fatal beam over the foaming water stood the devil himself, with all the terrors peculiar to his dark majesty. Great burning eyes rolled like wheels of flaming fire in his awful face, a shaggy-haired hide clothed the spirit of the bottomless pit, and the fearful claws were extended to seize his prey.

With trembling hand the elder of the two strangers produced the cards; but however falsely he shuffled them the death-card fell to him, and he began to quake, and grew as pale as the chalk of the wall.

Under the pretext that something had been omitted, the stranger shuffled again; but, to his terror, the death-lot fell, not upon Schlosser, but his own friend.

"The third time it will surely fall on the fellow," thought the stranger to himself, and began under all sorts of excuses to shuffle again.

The foul fiend raised himself to his greatest height, breathing flames of fire from mouth and nostrils, and cried in a hollow, smothered voice, like the sound of distant thunder: "Only once more can ye draw lots, no more. Over that person there," pointing to Schlosser, "I have no power; he is defended, by a plant which he carries on his person, from every danger!"

The two old sinners turned paler than ever, and

looked despairingly at each other; but the devil waved his hand, and they drew lots for the third time. The lot fell on him on whom it had fallen the first time.

Like a tempest Satan threw himself on the despairing man, seized him with his claws, rose with him in the air, and tore him to pieces.

With swelling breast, breathless, Schlosser till now had looked on all that had passed; but at this fearful sight the last spark of firmness failed him; he closed his eyes and sank lifeless on the ground.

When he awoke he was lying before the entrance to the cave; near him a sack filled with beaten gold and silver.

He looked in vain for his companion, who must have already gone away, if the terror caused by the awful fate of his friend had not killed him.

Schlosser was as if paralysed, and could scarcely drag himself to the village near by.

He, however, soon recovered, moved from Osterhagen to Andreasburg, where he built a handsome house, and never forgot that it was through his wife's forethought that wealth and happiness had been won.

The Bell-Founder of Stolberg.

THE traditions of the apprentice's pillar in Roslin Chapel, and of the bell-founder in Breslau, bear a strong resemblance to this of Stolberg.

There was once a bell-founder in Stolberg who was

a master worthy of honour, skilled in counsel and deed.

He had already cast many bells, yellow and white, the poem tells us, for churches and chapels, to the praise and glory of God.

And his bells rang so full, so clear, and pure in tone ; he cast love and faith in with the metal.

And Stolberg desired also a work from his hand, and the master employed every means to produce a perfect bell for his place of residence.

But it was as if the Evil One had a hand too in the work, for the cast was a perfect failure.

Vexed, he threw the bell aside, commanded his sixteen-years-old apprentice to prepare everything for a new cast on a certain day, so soon as he returned, and then departed to visit his father, who was also a bell-founder, to relate his failure and ask his advice.

The thoughtful apprentice reflected unceasingly on the cause of the failure of his so skilful master in the last bell.

After long speculation he discovered the cause, sprang up joyfully, worked day and night, and soon the bell stood without a flaw before the youth's delighted eyes.

His heart beating high with joy, he went to meet his master, and found him sitting on a stone resting from the fatigue of his long walk. This stone tradition still points out in the Steigethal, moss-grown, with a bell and a club hewn in it.

The apprentice could not keep his secret, and with a countenance shining with joy, told his master that he had already cast another bell, which was perfect, and of the sweetest tone.

Then the veins on the master's forehead swelled with shame ; rage and fury to find himself excelled by his pupil filled his usually mild heart.

He sprang from the stone, seized his cane, and gave the youth such a powerful blow on the head that he sank bleeding, with glassy eyes, in the grass.

The master fled as if chased by the Furies.

His anger cooled at the sight of the blood ; fearful pangs of conscience seized the strong man, he repented his rash deed, turned hurriedly back, hoping he might yet quench the stream of blood, and save the unhappy boy.

He had soon reached him, but no help was possible Despairing he fled.

Unsettled and a fugitive like Cain, he wandered the whole night in the forest, and when the morning dawned he had made his decision.'

He returned to Stolberg, presented himself before the tribunal, accused himself of his crime, and demanded punishment.

Deep was the regret, but blood demands blood, and he heard his sentence of death with unmoved composure.

14

The Colt's Cave.

DURING the Seven Years' War the soldiers stole all the horses.

A farmer concealed a handsome colt·in a cave in the Steigethal, or valley of the Steige, and fed it with great care.   After the departure of the enemy he hastened to the cave to take home the animal, but it had grown so much it could no longer go through the entrance, and he was compelled to kill it.   And the cave is called the Colt's Cave unto this day.

Legend of St. Christopher.

IN the Goslar Cathedral, of which now but a small remnant remains, once existed a colossal wooden statue* of this renowned Saint with the Christ-Child on his back.

St. Christopher once walked from Goslar to Halberstadt and Harzburg, and on the way shook on the ground a pea which had got into his shoe.

The pea grew, and became the sandstone rock called the Clus.†

The interior of the rock was hewn into a chapel to the Virgin, which was a shrine of great celebrity.

A Schloss once stood on the Clus, traces of which are still to be seen.

* There is such a statue still to be seen in Cologne Cathedral.

† *Clus*—Pronounced Cloos.

The Maiden's Cave in the Spatenberg, near where once stood the Spatenburg.

A YOUNG citizen of Sondershausen had, although honest, industrious, and skilful, fallen into great embarrassment.

Merciless creditors threatened with seizure; entire ruin stared him in the face; he saw himself already in fancy with wife and children abandoned to bitter want.

He took a walk into the country in order to seek relief for his oppressed heart for a few short hours.

Soon he was alone with his sorrow in the wood solitude.

He climbed the Göldner, till he had reached the summit of the Spatenberg, where the green-grass carpet and the shade of the old beeches invited him to a short repose.   -

He might have perhaps given expression to his trouble in loud lamentations.

However that may be, he at last prepared to go farther, when suddenly he observed a lovely maiden, who, clad in mourning garments, and weeping, sat on a moss-grown stone at the entrance to the Jungfernloch, or Maiden's Cave.

His sympathy at this sight was awakened in proportion to his own melancholy.   He could not restrain himself from approaching the graceful figure, and inquiring the cause of her grief.

She, however, was of opinion that her sorrow was much too great to permit of her troubling any one else with it, and declared she could only find a mitigation of her woe in drying up the tears of others.

She told him she had, unseen, perceived what troubled him, and it afforded her soul sweet comfort to know that she could help him.

After she had made this statement to the astonished man, she bade him follow her into the cave.

When they had gone through several dark, gloomy passages, they entered a wonderfully lighted chamber, in the centre of which stood a chest filled with gold and treasures, from which the maiden's companion, at her command, must take as many pieces of money as were sufficient for relief from his embarrassment.

At the same time he must solemnly promise that at the expiration of a year, at a certain hour, he will return the same sum to the same place, because, as a result of his failing to do so, she herself would suffer great injury.

He promised, and the maiden dismissed him.

Of course he was now freed from his anxiety and distress, and from this day everything he undertook prospered.

Not only was he able to satisfy all the demands of his creditors, but also at the stated time, agreeably with his promise, to return the received loan.

But he could not go in his every-day dress to his benefactress, and the untruthful tailor neglected to deliver the red Sunday coat as promised.

At last he determined, though he had failed to reach the spot at the fixed hour, not to fail in the day.

As he climbed the Burgweg—castle road—it seemed to him that the tops of the beeches sighed mournfully. He drew near to the cave with painful apprehensions.

No maiden was to be seen. He entered the cave, and found himself at last in the lighted chamber.

But what must he see? The benevolent maiden lay on the ground dying, her countenance distorted with sorrow and pain.

Dreadful gloom enveloped the frightened man. Only the treasure in the chest glittered dismally.

A long-drawn sigh trembled through the chamber. He threw the too-late-brought money, at the same time crossing himself, into the trunk, which immediately closed, and with the dead maiden disappeared.

An awful roaring arose. Benumbed with terror, he fled from the chamber, that fell in behind him, and through the passages, that seemed to him suddenly falling into ruins.

A tumbling stone struck him so violently on the heel that he was always obliged to wear slippers after, and from that day he never recovered his spirits.

The Three Brothers of Zellerfeld.

THERE once lived three brothers in Zellerfeld who were hunters. They went together one day hunting to the Schalk, when the youngest saw three partridges, and shot one of them.

He thought he had struck the bird, but it flew away, and he followed it to the top of the mountain where it disappeared.

The young hunter searched the spot carefully where the bird had vanished, and found an opening, which he marked, and then went back and called his two brothers.

All three entered the opening, and came soon to a large room containing a well-served meal on the table, and chairs placed ready.

The three seated themselves, ate, drank, and found all excellent.

After they had partaken of the repast, three beautiful ladies in rich attire entered, and told the brothers they were accursed and doomed to remain forever under the earth. But if they would remain there three years without seeing the light of day, they would be released.

The ladies promised them the best table during the time, and conducted them to see their treasures, and pointing out three casks filled with gold, promised each one.

They also told them they must now become black, and would only visit them once a year, exhorted the brothers to firmness, and left them.

At the end of the first year they returned ; they were become somewhat whiter.

At the next visit, at the end of the second year, they were grown still whiter. They exhorted the brothers earnestly to perseverance, and again left them.

The first half of the third year passed happily, but in the last half the eldest brother grew impatient, and asked : "Why should we remain here any longer ?"

But the younger reminded them of their promise. At last the second brother became undecided and restless, and finally the two resolved to remain no longer.

They threatened to murder the youngest if he would not accompany them, and to save his life he yielded to their entreaties.

At the proposal of the eldest, they took as much of the gold as they could carry with them.

They reached Zellerfeld with their wealth, agreed to keep all a secret, and began to live in luxury, each taking to himself a wife.

The two eldest brothers soon squandered all, but the youngest avoided their extravagance.

The two elder, having lost all, determined to return to the treasure in the mountains, and compelled the younger to go with them.

They entered the familiar chamber with the table and chairs, but all was changed.

Every object was draped in black, and on the table stood three mourning lamps.

The three ladies entered, now coal-black, and silent, and sad ; they were followed by three men, who cried, pointing to the eldest brother, " Thou perjured rascal !" seized him, quartered him, and packed him in a barrel, likewise the second.

The youngest looked on in terror; but the ladies exclaimed, " Thou art a true friend, and innocent. Take what thou wilt and go home. But we must remain here until we find three rescuers."

The Raven of Clausthal.

A GENTLEMAN in Clausthal had a raven and a maid-servant.

The raven carried off all the silver spoons, and suspicion fell on the poor girl. She was tried, and under torture confessed she had stolen them.

She was executed, but before her death declared her innocence.

Soon after new eave-troughs were put on the gentleman's house, and the spoons were all found where the raven had hidden them.

The Bergmönch* and Wilder Mann.†

THERE are numerous traditions of the Bergmönch in the mining districts.

He is always seen in the dress of a master-miner, with a silver mine-lamp in his hand.

It is said he was a master-miner, and begged to be permitted to inspect the mines until the Judgment Day. The Monk's valley—Mönchsthal—near Clausthal, was his favourite retreat.

In St. Andreasberg the tradition is, he was a monk who sought to open the mines there, but failed.

According to this tradition, he completed nearly the entire canal at the base of the Rehberg,‡ called the Rehberger Graben, which conveys all the water to St. Andreasberg for the working of the Samson mine, but became bankrupt through the undertaking.

Many wild tales are told of his bringing aid to the miners, and to the poor and distressed, and of his severity towards the wrong-doer.

In the mining town Wildemann there is a tradition of a wild man who gave the place its name.

Once a robber from the Thuringian Forest lived here in a cave with a wild woman; they were clothed with moss and the branches of fir-trees.

The knight Claus, founder of Clausthal, once saw

---

* *Bergmönch*—mountain monk ; or, as employed here, miner-monk.

† *Wilder Mann*—wild man.   ‡ *Rehberg*—stag mountain.

this wild man on the Wildmann's Cliffs, with a fir-tree, torn up by the roots, in his hand, and a bear on his back.

The Nimrod of the Rehbergerklippe.*

A LEGEND of this gloomy wild mountain, at the base of which one drives from Clausthal to St. Andreasberg, lingers still with a poetic charm on and around its rocky walls, and is in harmony with its decorations.

In the grey primeval days dwelt in this savage wilderness a mighty hunter, hard and rough as the rocks on which his house stood.

Hunting was his pleasure and passion, and daily he ranged, with his men, the wood, which resounded with the barking of dogs and the notes of the horn, which filled the clefts and caves of the rocks and mountains with a thousand-voiced echo.

Not even the peace of the Sabbath could check the delight of the huntsman in the chase, or restrain him from the continued persecution of the animals of the woods.

A pious hermit admonished him frequently, and entreated him not to disturb God's peace of the holy day with his tumult and noise; but the sportsman closed his ears to the warnings of the old man, and

* *Rehbergerklippe*—cliff of the stag mountain.

the hermit returned to his hermitage accompanied by the scornful derision of the ungodly hunter.

The evening of an October Sunday fell softly over the mountains; the tops of the fir-trees, rocks and mountains were bathed in the golden splendour of sunset; on the whole scene lay deep silence, only the waves of the Oder murmured in the distance their eternal song; only the timid game left its secure hiding place, stole cautiously with light, slow steps out of the thickets, and sought the spicy plants or the cooling spring.

Then resounded suddenly the noise of the hunt in the distance; the game so peacefully refreshing itself fled in terror, and the tumult increased every instant.

A snow-white stag flew with the rapidity of the wind over the mountains, pursued by the hunters on foot and on horseback, and surrounded by the barking pack of hounds.

The ground thundered beneath their horse-hoofs, and the mountains rang with the wild "hallohs!" of the riders, the cracking of whips, and the clashing of weapons.

The hunted stag groaned and escaped his pursuers with his last strength.

The noble animal stood breathless on the brink of the abyss which is called after him the Stag Cliff, and started back in fear and trembling from the black gulf.

And louder and nearer thundered the wild call of

the hunters, the hunting horns came fearfully near, and as the hounds would seize their prey, the stag in deadly terror, made the leap into the frightful deeps

And there arose a singular light, a dazzling splendour shone around the hunted animal, and unseen hands bore it softly below into the secure valley.

But the hunters, with horse and hound, were driven by magical power to follow the stag.

From the rocky cliff the whole company leaped into the depths, and huge blocks of granite and high pines sank after them and buried their mangled bodies in eternal night.

From that time it has been a haunted spot, full of untold horrors, and the wanderer hastens by in fear when darkness is closing in on the mountains.

And at midnight when the death-owl hoots and soars over the vale on heavy wing, and the fantastic moonlight transforms the dry trunks of the trees into grey spirits of the night, the giant forms of hunters brush past, and the firs whisper, then roar, and a smothered crash rushes on like the swelling waves of the sea.

The Tanzteich* bei Zorge.

ON the spot now covered by the Tanzteich once stood a stately Schloss with lofty walls and battlements.

A rich knight, whose name has been drowned in

* *Tanzteich*—dance pond.

the stream of time, dwelt in it in luxury and splendour.

Every dawn brought a new festival, and even night was turned into day ; but neither discipline nor virtue ruled in the brilliant assemblages of his numerous guests.

Once the lord of the castle gave a brilliant entertainment. The merriment of the guests rang out into the night ; in the wildest dance mingled men and women, youths and maidens, and loud music smothered the rolling thunder which could be heard in the distance.

And the night grew darker, and the waves of the Zorge murmured with a hollow moan, and the flowers grew wet with dew.

The heavens gathered blackness, the water of the river seemed to sing a death-song, and the flowers on its banks to weep.

Then the lightnings covered the mountains with flames, making the darkness still more terrible.

An old man stole softly and slowly up to the castle. His garments betrayed the greatest poverty, but his countenance was noble, and his thin locks were dripping with rain.

He entered, but the servants paid no attention to him, but sat drinking.

He mounted the stone stairway, and reached the ball-room, where knights and ladies whirled in the dance regardless of the storm.

He did not venture to enter, but stood timidly near the door, hoping that some one might take pity on his condition.   He did not stand long unobserved.

The master himself perceived him, but his heart was not touched with pity.

With a countenance red with anger, he pounced upon the trembling man, thrust him out of his humble posture, and cried in a voice of thunder, "Insolent beggar! how couldst thou dare to enter my castle ? Thou shalt pay dearly for thy impudence, and go down more quickly than thou camest up !"

And he seized him, dragged him to a window, and threw him, amid the laughter of the guests, into the depths below the castle.

But the beggar stood suddenly in the midst of a wonderful light, and cried in an awful voice, before which all merriment died, and the hot blood turned to ice : "Cursed are ye who despise the poor, and give them over to death ; cursed be this spot with all your pleasure and luxury ; ye shall sink this very hour in night and darkness !"

And lo ! scarcely were the words uttered, when a hissing flash of lightning, like a fiery serpent, pierced the castle, a fearful clap of thunder followed, the earth opened, the castle sank in the hidden deeps, and was seen no more.

Only the lonely wanderer hears in the stillness of the night a gloomy noise like distant merriment and shouting, mingled with smothered groans and a horrible dirge.

The Dwarfs of the Sachsenstein.

ON the spot where the few houses forming Dorf Neuhof now stand lay, centuries ago, a farm-house built of stone and ornamented with oddly-twisted chimneys.

A green meadow valley lay before the house, on which fat, comfortable-looking cows were grazing; well-scoured milk-pails hung on the garden fence, fruit-trees were trained on the house-walls, a powerful dog lay basking in the glowing sunshine before the door; from the well-populated barn-yard one heard an animated conversation among the feathered tribes, where a peacock was chairman, and made short emphatic speeches, and a turkey-cock filled the office of crier; in short, all bore the stamp of wealth and comfort.

And yet the owner of all, Herr Adam Neubauer, walked discontentedly up and down his room.

His sharp eye had long observed that pilfering hands had laid hold of his field-products, and it had pained him excessively that one would steal from him, for he had never permitted the needy to depart with empty hands; but in the last night so much had been stolen from his pea-field that his hitherto silent displeasure broke forth in expressions of anger.

"Anna," said he to his wife, a blonde of perhaps thirty years, with soft features and gentle dove eyes, "thou knowest I am patience itself, but that is too bad—that is too bad. The people take advantage of my forbearance and kindness, and it is time to let them see that I can also be angry. The first one I catch stealing, if he has only taken one ear, shall be so punished that he will forget to come again, thou mayest depend on it!"

"But, dear husband," replied Frau Anna, in a gentle voice, for she had not seen her husband so excited for a long time, "do not excite thyself so. Certainly it is vexatious when wicked men lay hands on our property; but as all the people of the earth are not purely honourable, if thou wilt appoint guards, thou wilt soon have the pleasure of seeing the thieves face to face."

"It is just that that makes me so angry," answered Neubauer—"that all the appointed sentinels do not help in the least. Since eight days, our servants, well hidden, have watched; but no one has shown himself, and nevertheless as much has been stolen as before. What is to be done?"

Anna heard with surprise this puzzling communication, and after many suppositions on the subject she went out shaking her head, to direct household matters, and Adam remained alone in his vexation.

The evening of the same day the heavens had greatly changed. It had been sultry all day, and now dark, silver-bordered clouds rose over the Harz, united and formed a colossal black wall.

It grew darker and darker. Hollow rolled the distant thunder, the dazzling lightnings flamed, and great drops fell. Fearfully raged the storm in the tops of the firs and beeches, and drove dust and gravel in wild whirls up the mountain path, on which now a wanderer, with hair wildly blowing in the wind and fluttering garments, descended.

Not a ray of light pierced the clouds save the fire of the lightning, followed ever more quickly by the deafening claps of thunder;* in torrents the clouds now poured their streams on the mountains, the firm rocks seemed to quake to their foundations; it was as if the *Dies Iræ* were come.

Shivering with the cold rain, the wanderer hastened to the house of Adam Neubauer, which, by the flashes of the lightning, he had long perceived in the distance.

He had to wait long before his knocking was heard, for the storm turned the weathercock with a rattling noise, shook the tiles of the roof, and threw at intervals an open-hanging shutter violently to and fro.

At last the hospitable door was opened, and the honest house-father received the stranger—a perhaps sexagenarian of lofty stature, powerful frame, with a shrewd countenance and snow-white hair—with the greatest readiness; and Frau Anna hurried away to look out dry garments from her husband's wardrobe,

* No word-painting could describe a thunder-storm on the mountains. The writer witnessed such a storm when driving up the Brocken. Just in front of the carriage the lightning rent a large fir to ribbons, and it was almost impossible for the horses to advance.

15

and to order from larder and cellar a strengthening, refreshing repast.

The stranger soon found himself comfortable, and Herr Adam took so much pleasure in his guest that he became confidential by the first glass, and speedily related to him his losses in the fields with all particulars.

The guest listened attentively, and then went out for a few minutes to look at the neighbourhood.

He shortly returned, took his staff, thanked Neubauer for the hospitable reception, and said: "Ye were to me as to a near relative, me a perfect stranger; hence, hear as a reward my counsel. If ye would discover the thieves who rob your fields, go out at midnight and strike about in the air with a willow rod, and ye will soon see the cunning rascals. And now farewell!"

He disappeared through the door and left his host in the greatest amazement at his odd advice.

True, his astonishment gave place to scornful laughter, and Adam concluded to himself not to permit himself to be made a fool of; but as he found, several hours afterwards, that a new robbery had been committed, he decided, nevertheless, to follow the stranger's advice.

It was a glorious still night. In the shadows sang the queenly nightingale. The full moon shone in the cloudless heavens.

The precipitous wall of the Sachsenstein stood in

shadowy contrast against the star-powdered blue, and seemed in the magical moonlight as if silvered.

Herr Adam stood early in his peafield watching, and as the bell in the neighbouring Sachsa rang out the midnight hour, he struck, as the stranger had advised, with the willow rod he had brought with him up and down in the air, and soon saw, with the greatest amazement, two tiny beings, who, with folded hands and terrified mien, looked up to him.

If they had taken advantage of Adam's surprise, they might have made their escape ; but fear and terror rooted them to the spot till he had recovered himself, seized them with a firm hand, and asked in a stern voice who they were, and where they came from.

"Ah !" replied one of the little creatures, " we are poor dwarfs, who house there in the Sachsenstein, and never do anybody any harm. But hunger drove us this time to take some peas from your field. We beg you to forgive us, and we will make good the damage we have done."

"Of course you will," answered Herr Neubauer, who observed closely the little men, of whose acts and deeds he had already heard so much; "but the reckoning will be large, for you have long done mischief to my property. First of all, tell me how it happened that my watchers did not discover you, nor I myself till I struck with the willow rod ?"

" We possess *Nebelkappen*," * said one of the two

* *Nebelkappen*—magical caps ; literally, fog caps. Like the *Tarn-kappe* in the *Nibelungenlied*, that renders the wearer invisible.

dwarfs, "which render us invisible to the human sight. You knocked them off our heads with the willow rod, and then we became visible. Will you permit us to look for them ?"

"Certainly not," returned Adam. "Do you fancy I shall be so stupid as to put the means into your hands of escaping ?   No, no; you follow me into my house, and will not regain your freedom till you have paid me!"

The dwarfs wept, and pleaded so pitifully to be released, that Adam's mild heart grew soft; but a glance at his field hardened it again, and he took his trembling prisoners home with him.

The next morning the two guilty dwarfs were examined, who related that they, governed by a king, had dwelt for untold ages in the caves of the Harz, more especially in the Sachsenstein, and had been happy; but now subterranean floods and landslips had caused them heavy losses, so that they had been compelled to appropriate the possessions of men for their necessities.

They would, however, never again venture to do so, and once more expressed their willingness to pay for the damages they had caused, and begged to know the sum demanded of them.

"If I should reckon all the mischief you have caused," said Herr Adam, "a pretty long account would be the result; but I demand only the value of the peas, and if you pay me three Gulden I will set you at liberty."

The dwarfs were well satisfied with this demand, but protested that they had neither money nor articles of value with them, and begged permission to go and bring the money.

But Adam could not be induced to permit this. Even to keep one as hostage, and allow the other to depart, he absolutely refused.

" Well, then, give us a rose-leaf and a pin," begged the dwarfs. " We will write to our king, and he will undoubtedly at once release us from our painful position."

After some reflection, Adam permitted his wife, who looked at him with beseeching eyes, to bring the required objects.

As soon as the dwarfs had bescribbled the rose-leaf, they handed it to him with directions to carry it to the Sachsenstein, and blow it in through one of the crevices, and a reply would speedily follow.

The features of the little creatures grew cheerful as they heard that their odd letter had been posted as directed, and they became merry and contented, although the day passed without anything happening for their release.

But when night came on, and the moon and stars shone in a clear sky, the door of the room opened suddenly in which Adam sat with his prisoners, and a troop of handsome dwarfs, neatly dressed, entered.

At their head walked the king himself, in gold and purple, and wearing a sparkling crown.

As soon as the prisoners beheld their sovereign they knelt reverently before him, and remained in that humble position until the monarch motioned them to rise. The presence of the pygmean ruler was indeed so commanding, that Herr Neubauer himself involuntarily uncovered his head before him.

At last the king broke the silence, and said: "Ye have made two of my subjects prisoners, and I am come to interest myself on their behalf, for they are otherwise good men, who now only through pressure of circumstances have been led astray to do you damage. Moreover, that ye may see that I approve of your demand, I will cause ten times as much to be paid."

His Majesty signed to one of his suite, who immediately approached, and counted from a bag which he carried under his arm thirty shining new Gulden, and laid them on the table.

Adam opened his eyes on seeing so much money. He had already decided in his mind to set the delinquents free without ransom, as soon as he had frightened them a little.

Surprised at the royal generosity, he at once proclaimed to the prisoners their liberation, who sprang up with eyes shining with joy, fell at the feet of the Dwarf King, and thanked him for their freedom in the most touching expressions of gratitude.

After the king had graciously raised them from their knees, he turned again to Adam, and said: "I thank you that you have not harmed these poor people, and notify you that in future you have nothing to fear from us, for on St. John's Eve I shall march from this place over the bridge with my subjects. Already for a long period the subterranean water floods have threatened to drive us from the Sachsenstein, which we have inhabited so long, and I shall leave only a few of my people, in order not to wholly lose this ancient possession; from them, however, you will suffer no molestation."

The sovereign bowed graciously and departed, attended by his train. The two released prisoners followed with joyful gestures, hand in hand.

St. John's Eve, Frau Anna and her husband, full of curiosity, together with the servants, hid themselves near the bridge to see the dwarfs march over.

Scarcely had the darkness come on, when the procession appeared in sight, a well-ordered company, and the concealed heard their march till the rising of the sun, and the noise thereof was like the light trampling of a flock of sheep.

Since that time nothing has been seen or heard of the dwarfs, and not only here but everywhere they are vanished; but their memory lives in the mouth of the people, and when the icy north wind blows, and the snow beats against the windows, young men and maidens gather around the fire in confidential chat, and to the rattling of the wheel tell of the deep clefts of the mountains, where in eternal night the dwarfs once held their weddings, and where gnomes and nymphs and fairies in darkness dwell.

The Burggeist* of the Haarburg.

THE mountain called the Haarburg, which has a summit of only small circumference, bore in a long-forgotten time a fortress, which, like most ancient castles, consisted of a single strong tower.

In its walls were housed the first lords of Wernigerode. But the mountain on which the present Schloss Wernigerode stands was adorned only with the primeval forest.

For centuries the occupants of the Haarburg felt themselves happy in the grey giant tower, until a Graf Bodo dwelt in it. He was the father of a numerous progeny, and the tower grew too small for all the children and domestics, and he often felt a wish to have a more capacious dwelling.

An addition to the tower was not to be thought of, in consequence of the small space on the mountain summit ; and one evening, as he sat with his wife before the entrance to the Haarburg, and looked out on the beautiful landscape, he said to her, pointing toward the mountain where the present castle stands :

" What thinkest thou ? Would it not be well if we could live yonder ? The mountain has plenty of space ; and there would be room to build spacious

---

* *Burggeist*—patron spirit.

salons and chambers, and even a chapel, and a single
moat around the whole; then we should be able to
entertain our friends, as many as could come. What
is thy opinion ?"

The lady of the castle quite agreed with her husband. They conversed long on the subject, and only
separated as darkness began to settle over the vales
and mountains, and the benevolent Luna hung out
her silver lamp.

The night was lovely, and the Countess could not
rest or sleep. She opened the window, and gazed at
the shining moon, sank in thought, and did not
observe that the moments fled swiftly, and midnight
and the owls hovered over her head.

Then, out of a corner of the chamber, with light,
noiseless steps, issued an odd being, a little man, with
an old, wrinkled face, a long grey beard, but with not
disagreeable features.

His attire consisted of a grey coat and a pointed
hat, and he carried a staff.

Silently the figure approached the thinking, dreaming Countess, on whose form the soft moonlight fell,
and then twitched gently her garment with his tiny
hand.

Alarmed, the Countess turned round, but lost all
fear so soon as she beheld the form of the grey man.

She had recognized the Burggeist, who appeared
seldom, but always brought happiness with him, and
inquired in a gentle voice :

" What wilt thou from me, thou good spirit ? "

" I saw thee at such a late hour sitting in troubled thought," replied the patron spirit, in a melodious voice, " and came to ask the cause of thy sorrow. What trouble lies so heavily at thy heart ? "

" No sorrow troubles me," said the countess, smiling, " Only a wish moved my soul."

" And what might that be ? " inquired the spirit with strained attention.

" My husband," replied the Countess, " would wish this fortress on that spacious mountain opposite. He declares that we cannot live longer here ; and I must say, after due reflection, he is perfectly right."

" Does it no longer please thee here ? " asked the dwarf, with a quick-clouding face. " Ye men are right difficult to please ! Thy ancestors have dwelt here for ages, happy and contented, and now ye would forsake the tower that has sheltered thy race so long. Ye are very ungrateful. If I had known that that was all that troubled thee, I should not have left my hiding-place. But it is already late ; seek thy couch and rest well ! "

The spirit vanished, and the Countess followed his advice ; but troubled dreams sported around the head of the sleeping lady, and fantastic scenes passed before her fancy.

It seemed as if she saw the dwarf from her window go out at the entrance of the tower, large as a giant, striking in the air with his hands all sorts of odd signs and motions, and with a powerful voice she heard him cry: "Slide on ! Slide on !"*

And hardly were these words out of his mouth when the Haarburg was raised on unseen hands from its foundations high in the air, so high that the Countess was seized with giddiness, and awoke in terror.

As she opened her eyes it was already light ; but the sun had not yet risen above the mountains, so she could only have slept a short time, but felt so much strengthened and refreshed that she rose, dressed, and went to the window to enjoy the fresh morning. But who shall describe her amazement when she saw the town of Wernigerode directly beneath, and on closer observation found that the old tower Haarburg had been moved in the night to the mountain where her husband had so earnestly desired to have it.

As soon as her first astonishment had passed, the Countess hastened to her still slumbering husband, led him to the window, and feasted her eyes on his boundless astonishment and joy.

Filled with gratitude, she called the benevolent dwarf, to thank him ; but he did not answer the summons, and has never been seen in the new Schloss.

* " *Rücke dich ! Rücke dich !*"

The Three Wood-Fairies.

THE great plain north of the Harz mountains was not always the smiling, fruitful tract of land the eye now beholds.

A great lake covered a large portion of it; the ground around this lake was swampy and unfruitful, and dense forests shut out the sunlight.

But the deep shadows of these woodlands, where the foot of man seldom wandered, this sacred stillness, undisturbed by the noise and bustle of human life, was notwithstanding peopled.

Creatures of tender form and rare beauty—not so ethereal as the air, not so material as man—danced lightly, as if borne by the breezes, through the woods, which were their possession, intimately interwoven with their existence, for they grew with the trees which they inhabited, and drooped and died with them.

When the moon mounted her blue throne, and cast her pure silvery glance over the silent and noble forest, it was as if a light shiver fell on the trees, as if they became animated, and assumed the forms of maidens, who in the pale light skipped upon the mountains, or descended to the lake or the Bode, to visit their neighbours the mermaids, still and innocent as themselves, who swam the light waves radiant in the smile of Queen Luna.

But as time went on these pleasant reunions were

interrupted by the human race, which penetrated the forests, mercilessly cut down everything that stood in the way of its selfish ends, and made these peaceful regions the stage of its vain ambitions and aims, never dreaming that with every tree that was hewn down a life more pure and beautiful than its own was destroyed.

Soon the joy at these nightly assemblies was changed to sorrow, and when the moonlight called the fairy forms of wood-nymphs and mermaids into life, they wept together over their vanished sisters and friends, and not one was sure that the following day the same sad fate would not be her destiny.

A powerful Kaiser was come into the district with a vast retinue and an army, had built himself a Burg on the banks of the Bode, and bestowed the land on his followers, who were to cut down trees, drain swamps, and transform the wilderness into a fruitful plain.

The woods gave place speedily to a bare tract, and the maiden circle grew ever smaller. There, on the mountain west of Thale, where in its bosom the antediluvian giant animal skeletons were found, an old warrior had received permission from the Kaiser to clear the land.

He toiled unweariedly, dug the soil, felled the trees one after the other, till of the sacred grove only three trees were left standing.

"Now, only these three trees left," thought he to himself, stretched himself wearily in the grass to rest a minute and strengthen himself for the last stroke; but fatigue overcame him, so that he sank into a deep sleep, and only awoke when the moon and stars shone in the heavens.

Then he saw three maidens sitting under the green roof of a maple tree, silent and mournful; their eyes were wet as if dewdrops hung in the drooping eye-lashes; they uttered complaining words in soft tones like the rustling of the night wind in the leaves.

"Let us take leave of each other," lisped softly the voice of one; "our time is come. When the rosy dawn awakes he will come who cut down our sisters; and as they are fallen, so must we. Desolate will be the spot that saw us so oft united in joy, lonely the moon-light that shone on our dance. The nymphs of the lake and the mountain stream will look out for us, longing for our coming, and ask, 'Where are our friends of the mountain? Why do they not descend when the Queen of the stars illuminates our palace?' Happy sisters, ye are as yet safe from our mourn-ful fate, for ye are secure in your retreat from the barbarian!"

"Weep not, sister!" said another, with light moan-ing; "weep not over our inevitable destiny. To see that we must die grieves me not, for all our beloved are gone on before us; but that we are the last of our race, and our line becomes with us extinct, that it is that fills my heart with woe.

"That our race might continue I would live on, and

if I could appear in person to him who will come in the morning with his axe to annihilate us, I would entreat him for the blessing of life, and he would not refuse my entreaty.

"But only night gives us being comprehensible to men; the day confines us stiff and without form in our narrow house."

"Ah! if we could only appear to him!" added the third; "if we could only appear and beg him for life, we should not plead in vain; 1 have seen him mourn too, have heard him lament the beautiful forest.

"And what benefit would it be to him to destroy us also? What benefit has it been to him that he has destroyed our sisters? Will the products of this soil repay the labour of tillage? But we would gladly, though invisible, help him to cultivate the land during the hours when we have a form, if he would take pity and spare the last of a great race."

The old soldier, who had listened in surprise to this singular conversation, could contain himself no longer.

"By the sword of my Kaiser!" he cried, springing to his feet, "cursed be the hand that should do you an injury, ye innocent beings.; destroy you I will not, no, but protect and defend you with my goods, blood, and life.

"But who are ye? Was it a dream that charmed my senses?"

Terrified, the maidens had vanished at his first words.

Now their voices resound from the trees as they reply to his question.

"No dream has deceived thee. Thou has seen the last of the wood-nymphs who adorn this mountain. If thou wilt protect them, so spare the trees of the wood that still stand; they will thank thee."

Dawn broke over the mountains, the voices were silent; they sighed in the morning wind, but the soldier could not understand the tones; at first he was inclined to hold all for a dream, but what he had heard stood so clear in his mind that he finally doubted no longer, and zealously defended the three trees.

On his dying bed he commended them to his sons, and charged them never to sell the land.

Long the fields near the three trees thrived above all others, and at night three maiden forms could be seen following the plough in the moonlight.

But alas! the trees and land came into the hands of an owner who held the story of the three wood-fairies for a fable, and he cut the trees down.

Since then the mountain has been barren and fruitless, and the three sisters have never been seen with the plough again.

The Shepherds' Towers.

TWO shepherds in Quedlinburg, father and son, poor but honest people, were once watching their flocks on the green meadows.

It was a lovely morning; the lambs played with the wild flowers, the birds sang so joyfully in the neighbouring wood, the breezes were so mild and odorous, that the hearts of the shepherds were filled with an unusual gladness, and they both began to play a sacred air on their reed pipes.

The bells of the royal convent began to ring, and their melodious harmonies penetrated the heart, powerful and irresistible as a voice from heaven.

"There is something glorious in such a solemn chime," said the elder shepherd to his son, who sat near him. "The tones seem to come down to us from the eternal heights, and remind us of our duty and our better home."

"It is indeed true," replied the younger. "The chimes possess an incomprehensible power over the mind, and awake the inner life to devotion and holy reflections; and I never look across to the towers whence those bold and fearless tones rise on the air, without seeing in them landmarks pointing to heaven."

"Oh, what a pity!" added the father, "that our new church in the New Town must stand so long without either tower or bells. What a pity that a work to God's honour must remain unfinished, while the rich

16

build palaces and heap up treasures. How willingly every poor person in the town would contribute, if thereby the edifice could only be completed. But without a special blessing from God, many years may pass away before the church is finished."

"Father!" cried the son, interrupting the conversation, " where are our dogs ? I don't see them by the flock, and still the faithful creatures have never yet left their post without our commands. What can have started them and allured them away ? Where shall we find them again ?"

"Yonder, my son !" said the father, whose eye had swept exploringly the neighbourhood, pointing toward the near forest. " I see them running as fast as possible toward the wood ; they scent game, no doubt, and are on the track."

And they both whistled, and called the dogs by name, but in vain, for the hitherto so obedient animals only turned their heads slightly at the sound of the well-known voices, and then continued their wild race.

Astonished at the unwonted disobedience, and anxious lest they might lose the dogs, the shepherds decided to follow them to the borders of the wood. The flock was feeding quietly in a meadow, and there was no danger of its wandering away.

The border of the wood was soon reached, but no trace of the dogs was to be seen. They had already penetrated the thick underbrush, and a stripe in the dewy grass showed the way they had taken.

"Wilt thou remain here, father, and watch that no wolf come out of the wood and scatter the flock?" said the son, and hurried on in the direction the dogs had taken.

The father remained standing, keeping his eyes on the lambs; but it was not long before he heard the missing dogs bark, and fancied he heard also the voice of his son.

He listened. He was not mistaken. The son called with all his might his father's name, who, terrified lest something dreadful had happened, hastened after the voice.

The way he had to take was perfectly strange to him, although he had often been in the same wood before; also the forest seemed very much altered; in the place of the young, slender trees, stood primeval, mighty oaks, and under their deep shades, through an opening in the trees, rose the grey dilapidated walls of a ruined church.

At the entrance to this church, half hidden by wild briars, trees, and ivy, he saw his son standing with a look of amazement and with an uncertain air, for he too had never discovered these ruins, and curiosity and fear of enchantment fought a sharp contest in his breast.

The arrival of the father, however, put an end to all fear, and after a short consultation, whether they should enter the desolate, ghost-like ruins, curiosity triumphed, so much the more, since they observed that the track of the dogs led through the bushes into the wall. With considerable effort they made their way through the rank weeds and thorns, and reached a high portal fallen in on one side. They went through it, and saw themselves surrounded by a dim twilight, since the openings in the arch ceiling were insufficient to light the interior, and the slender arched windows were so overgrown with ivy and other plants that they stood in a green night.

They could scarcely distinguish the spot where the altar had stood, and where masses of broken, scattered stones betrayed the fury of the storm that had destroyed it.

Approaching the spot, they were seized with trembling as they discovered an old crucifix in the wall, and, bending the knee, murmured a prayer.

A noise startled them ; looking around they perceived the dogs behind a portion of the broken altar, scratching and digging, without troubling themselves at the presence of their masters, as if they had been fastened by enchantment to the spot.

The shepherds approached the corner where they were scraping and pawing, and looked attentively at the hole growing every moment larger and deeper in the ground, and soon a sheet-iron chest became visible.

The dogs barked as if for joy at the discovery, stopped their work, and sprang barking from one shepherd to the other.

The shepherds set to work to lift out the chest, which they found tremendously heavy. It contained a mass of gold and silver coins with a stamp of a time long past.

Before they could recover from their astonishment, the dogs began again to scratch the ground in the same spot, and soon a second chest came to view, in which the shepherds found golden goblets, candlesticks, and other sacred vessels of immense value.

Not till now were the dogs satisfied, but as the second chest was opened they hurried back to the flock, and displayed an unwonted zeal to fulfil their duty.

The two shepherds repaired to the Abbess of the St. Servatius Convent in Quedlinburg, related what had occurred, and expressed a wish that two towers should be built on the Nikolai* church with the found treasure.

At the news of the wonderful discovery, half the town went out to the wood to see the spot where the treasure had been found. But no ruin was to be discovered; all was vanished without leaving a trace, and even the shepherds could not find the spot again.

If the treasure in their possession had not proved to the contrary, they would have held the whole thing for a dream.

The Nikolai church still stands, shaded by old lindens, and at its west end the shepherds' two towers.

* *Nikolai*—St. Nicholas.

The figures of the two shepherds and their dogs, hewn in the stone, still look down upon the ancient imperial city from these towers, where they were placed so many centuries ago as memorials of a somewhat unusual unselfishness.

The Treasure-hunters of the Sieberthal.

MANY centuries ago there lay in the valley of the little river Sieber, where now is the Long Meadow, copper-works.

A mass of scoria, the greater part of which has been employed on the *chaussée*, once marked the spot.

The owners of these works, who are said to have been very rich, together with the works vanished in a single night.

The following morning nothing remained to be seen but this huge heap of scoria.

It was said the owners had buried their treasure in it before their disappearance.

Soon after that event, a blue flame was seen every night between eleven and twelve on this heap of scoria, which a black man endeavoured to keep burning until midnight.

The report of a Goldfeuer* in the Sieberthal soon spread, and many saw the flame, but no one was bold enough to attempt to gain the treasure.

At last a man from Lonau, who had experience in

* *Goldfeuer*—Goldfire.

treasure-seeking, determined to attempt it, and engaged several workmen to assist him in the undertaking.

On the way to the spot he commanded his men: "Let no one speak while digging, or all is lost."*

They all promised, and gave him the hand as pledge.

Meanwhile they arrived at the spot, the work began, and soon they came to a huge cauldron filled with Holland ducats, which it was necessary to raise.

Just as they had raised the vessel to the surface they heard wheels.

The workmen paused and listened, when lo! a carriage appeared drawn rapidly by four doves.

The driver cried, "Guten Abend! Geht's gut?"† But not a soul replied.

Directly after came a fellow in a trough along the same road, saying hurriedly: "Shall I not also come?" and made the most desperate efforts to reach the dove-drawn carriage.

One of the workmen laughing, cried mockingly: "The poor devil must also drive!"

Hutsch! In an instant blue flame and cauldron had vanished!

The men stood gazing at each other with long faces, when instantly their hair turned grey, and they all soon died of grief and vexation.

---

* A search for all objects under enchantment must be conducted in silence. If one speaks, the charm is immediately broken.

† Good evening! How are you?

The Enchanted Maiden of the Zorge.

LIKE Princess Ilse, she sometimes appears as a serpent. On the Hohegeissberg, near the river Zorge, the White Maiden of the Staufenburg* is seen every seven years with a bunch of keys.

Once came a shepherd from Kloster Walkenried† and pastured his flock in the vicinity of the mountain.

Early in the morning the White Maiden stood on the cliffs, making her footprints in the rocks, and sang gaily.

When she had finished her song she descended to the shepherd, and asked him if he would rescue her from the enchantment.

He replied he would gladly if he could.

She told him she would return the next morning, at first in the same form, which he now saw, after which she would become a serpant. If he would kiss her in her serpent form, she would be free.

The shepherd promised solemnly.

The next morning she appeared again on the cliffs and sang as before.

When the sheep had all filed past, the maiden descended from the rocks, came to him as a serpent, and sprang upward toward him, that he might give her the serpent-kiss, but he turned aside in horror.

The serpent suddenly vanished with such a shriek

* The Staufenburg bei Zorge.

† The extensive ruins of Walkenried are the most picturesque convent ruins in North Germany. The style of architecture is that Gothic known as Early English.

of anguish that the shepherd was ever afterward perfectly deaf.

She is seen on the Staufenburg bei Zorge every seven years at Easter, with a bunch of keys and a Pomeranian dog white as snow.

She waits from eleven to twelve for a rescuer, and when the time is expired the dog barks.

This dog is said to have been her lap-dog before the curse.

There is a Harz legend that the Ascension took place from the mountain of the Staufenburg.

The Accursed Maiden of Lichtenstein.

NOT far from Lichtenstein is a spring, where once a shepherd rested always at noonday and watered his flocks.

One day, when he sat there as usual, a serpent came from under a stone and looked kindly at him.

At first he was seized with terror, but at last felt quite at home with her.

The second day she came again, from her head half in human form addressed the shepherd, and told him he must take courage the next day and kiss the serpent, when he would thereby become always fortunate and happy.

She came the third day from under the stone, crept up to him, and raised her head to kiss him.

At first he was filled with disgust, but taking courage he shut his eyes and kissed her.

And there stood before him no longer a serpent, but a beautiful girl, and more—a princess.

Then the shepherd forsook his sheep, went with the maiden to the king, who gave him the princess to wife.

The Great Hall in the Petersberg.

ONE day a child plucked a flower on the Petersberg, near Goslar, while playing.

Then the mountain opened, and the child came into a great hall, where many noble steeds neighed and tossed their proud heads, and the viands were served on gold and silver.

All who sat there wore golden crowns, and a silver plate was given the child to take home.

The parents of the child sought the *Wunderblume*, that they might also see this chamber, but failed.

These guests of the mountain are the old Kaisers who once held their Court in Goslar.

Spar-die-Müh.*

AT the north end of the Bergstadt † Lautenthal lies the Bielstein.

Below, at the north-west end of the town, the little river Innerste flows northward towards the Bielstein, and along its base.

* Spare the trouble.   † Mining town.

Above this bend in the stream, where it turns to flow along the base, only a few steps from the stream, is a cave called the Zwergloch, or Dwarf-cave.

The level place at the foot of the Bielstein bears the name of Spar-die-Müh.

In the cave dwelt in earlier times three dwarfs, who often lent the people of Lautenthal money, and also gold and silver plate for weddings and baptisms.

Now it happened once that these borrowed objects were not returned. So when the people came again to borrow, they heard a voice call, "Spar-die-Müh!"

And from that time the dwarfs declined to oblige the neglectful citizens in any way, and since then the place has been called Spar-die-Müh.

The Dwarf-King Hibich.

THE Hibichenstein, near Grund, consists of two colossal limestone cliffs leaning against each other, which are said to have been formed in the distant days when giants lived in the Hercynia Sylva,* from a pebble which a giant threw out of his shoe.

In the Hibichenstein dwelt dwarfs, who often attended the children in Grund.

Their King Hibich was ages old, with shaggy hair

* The Hercynia Sylva of the Romans was of greater extent than the Harz mountains. It included the Schwarzwald, Thuringen, Bohemia, and the Harz.

like a bear, a very wrinkled face, and a long ice-grey
beard, which possessed magical power.

He always carried a silver miner's lamp that shone
clear as the sun, and wore a golden crown.

Although so small, he could stretch himself much
larger.

Formerly his dwarf majesty was allowed to appear
in the upper world every five hundred years, but he is
no longer permitted to leave his subterranean abode.

He protected the forests, and played serious jokes
upon those who did them any injury.   But he was
benevolent and kind to those in distress who complained to him of their trouble.

Once a miner's wife whose husband had long lain
ill, went from Grund into the wood to gather cones for
the baker, who gave her bread for them.

When she had entered the forest, Hibich came to
her and asked : " What seekest thou here ? "

Then she told him all her want and distress, whereupon he gave her a plant to cure her husband, and
pointed out to her a spot where she would find plenty
of cones.

Arrived there, she could at first find none, but
directly the cones began to fall in showers from the
trees, not striking her, however, but all falling into
the basket.

When she lifted the basket to put it on her back,
she found it much heavier than the cones had ever
been before.

Returning to the spot where the King had first met her, he asked her if she had found cones. Then she told him what had happened, and the Dwarf-King revealed to her that his people had done it, and added the cones were pure silver.

He told her she was to take a sufficient number of them to make herself and her sick husband comfortable, and to provide for her children, and with the rest she was to build a church in Grund ; but by no means to forget the healing plant.

The sick man became "healthy as a fish " from the hour when he made use of this powerful herb.

In the forester's house in Grund lived in the olden days a forester who had lost his wife early, and had an only son, a good-hearted youth, only somewhat over-inquisitive and indiscreet.

One Sunday afternoon the forester's son, with his friend, the son of a miner, went into the wood for a walk.

As they reached the Hibichenstein they fell into a conversation concerning its height, and the miner's son said he should like to see the person who could climb to the top.

The other said that was nothing, he would do it; but his friend endeavoured to dissuade him from his purpose, saying no one who had climbed up could ever get down again, but was always found the next day broken to pieces at the base.

He was not be dissuaded, and climbed to the

summit, where he found a large level space, and began to dance and shout for joy, and called to his friend to climb up. But the other shook his head, and told him not to forget he had to come down.

Finally, when his joy had cooled, the forester's son decided to descend, but could not leave the spot, for the Dwarf-King Hibich held him enchanted to the rock for his presumption.

He called to his friend and entreated him to go and tell his father.

Then the forester came with his gun and would shoot his son down.

But as he was about to fire, came Hibich and demanded what he was going to do; and as he replied he was going to shoot his son down from the mountain, the King advised him not to attempt anything so foolish.

Again he took aim, when it began to thunder and lighten, and the rain poured down in torrents.

Night came on, and the forester was obliged to go home till morning.

Hardly had he gone when the dwarfs arrived, all in miners' dress, and each carrying a mine-lamp.

They had the most skilful ladders, which they placed one on the other, and now they held together as if they had been glued.

As soon as this ladder was ready, and reached the top of the Hibichenstein, a dwarf stood at each side and lighted the way.

The forester's son must now seat himself on the shoulders of the dwarf on the topmost rung of the ladder ; and see ! the ladder is wide enough to permit them to descend between the thick line of lamp-bearing dwarfs on either hand.

No sooner had they reached the base than dwarfs, lights, and ladder had vanished.

Then came the old Hibich, took him by the hand, and said : "As thou hast been on the summit of the Hibichenstein, and hast suffered so much anxiety and terror, thou shalt also see the Dwarf-King's castle."

Then they entered through a great arched door into the mountain, and the King conducted him to a large room, where stood chairs and a table.

The walls glittered with pure ore, the ceiling was a single piece of ponderous spar, white as the driven snow, and from it hung a chandelier of mountain crystal and precious stones.

The floor was strewed with branches of firs, and the panels shimmered with gold and jewels.

In the centre of this superb chamber stood a table of hematite ; before it a silver chair, upon which the Dwarf-King seated himself, and commanded his companion also to sit down.

Then he struck with a silver rapier upon the table of hematite, which produced a tone the sweetness of which was never heard before.

A thousand tiny female forms appeared in answer to the summons, bearing strawberries and raspberries ;

and while the King and his guest partook of the fruit, the dwarf maidens played the most delicious music.

Afterward costly wine was brought in silver goblets.

When the repast was ended, Hibich led his young visitor into an adjoining chamber, on one side of which was silver, on the other gold, and at the royal command, "Silver!" "Gold!" the forester's son must take of the metal named till he was laden with wealth.

Then the Dwarf-King said: "Wilt thou do me a favour? Namely, never to permit any one to shoot at birds on the Hibichenstein; for in this way bits of the rock are broken off.

"As long as the great Hibichenstein remains the great, my crown is secure; but so soon as it becomes the little Hibichenstein, I lose my crown, and can never appear on the earth again."

The youth promised, and Hibich conducted him to another chamber, where stood a delicious bed of fragrant moss, wished him Gute Nacht, and promised to wake him early.

The forester's son had slept but a short time, as it seemed to him, when he was waked up suddenly. It was early dawn, and he shivered, exclaiming, "How cold it is!"

He lay under a bush at the foot of the Hibichenstein, but all the gold and silver that the Dwarf-King Hibich had given him was heaped up beside him.

The King of Tipplers.

A LEGEND is told in Ellrich of an Earl von Klettenberg—not the devoted founder of the Huy Wald Abbey, whose forsaken wife built Kloster Walkenried.

The Earl rode one Sunday morning to Ellrich, as an invited guest to a grand banquet, where all the guests were to drink for a wager, the reward being a chain of gold.

They drank for hours, till all were *hors de combat* save four knights.

Three of these leaned against the wall, and only the Earl von Klettenberg stood upright; to him therefore, the victory was awarded.

He resolved to show himself to the people as the winner, and commanded his horse to be brought. Four of his attendants lifted the Earl into the saddle, and he rode through the village.

As he reached the St. Nicholas Church, he heard the chanting of vespers, rode through the open door into the church and spurred on his horse till he had ridden through the congregation, whose vesper-chant changed to terror and dismay.

But as he reached the steps of the altar, all the four horse-shoes fell off, and the horse and his rider sank to the ground.

The four huge horse-shoes were nailed to the church

17

door, where they remained for centuries, and the awful tale was oft related to trembling listeners.

At last a fire destroyed the church, and the four horse shoes are unhappily lost.

The Needle's Eye.

NEAR Kloster Ilfeld, close by the *chaussée*, stands on a mountain a huge boulder, which has a small hole through the centre.

All the servants from Nordhausen and the other surrounding places, when they drive into the forest the first time for wood, must creep three times through this hole—which is only done with difficulty; and as they creep in, and on the opposite side out, their comrades lash them with their whips.

If the new-comer will not indulge in this pastime, he must pay money.

The new pupils in the high school at Ilfeld must also, as a joke, creep through the Needle's Eye.

This stone a giant is said to have thrown out of his shoe.

Legend of St. Hubertus.

ST. HUBERTUS, the Patron Saint of the house of Anhalt, was a passionate lover of the chase.

One day, hunting in the old oak wood on the mountain Hubertushöhe, which lies between Gernrode and Ballenstedt, when about to shoot a deer, the Saint saw a cross rise from the head of the animal, when he immediately lost his passion for hunting, and according to the legend, "his only game became eternity and heavenly bliss."

Bathilde von Ballenstedt.

IN the Saxon Chronicles we are told that Ludwig, King of the Franks, took Schloss Ballenstedt, and carried away captive the fair daughter of the Earl of Askanien."

> " Dost thou not hear the snorting of steeds ?
>   Franks are marching through the wood
>   From the destroyed castle ; in their midst
>   The captive daughter.
>   Yes, like smothered tones of anger,
>   It rustles in the foliage of the oaks.
>   Sadly they shake their tops,
>   As if they knew of the robbery."

OPINIONS OF THE PRESS.

IN this neat little volume—dedicated by special permission to the young Queen Margherita, of Italy—Mrs. LAUDER has collected about seventy of the most interesting stories and legends current in Germany about the doings of dwellers in the great Harz Mountains in the olden times. The narratives of daring adventure, love, and wondrous doings, are related in appropriately simple terms, and these are sure to find many charmed readers, especially among young people. Though Mrs. LAUDER has not gone out of her way to adorn the stories—which was wise—she has supplied explanatory notes, which will be valued by readers unacquainted with Germany and the German language.—*Liverpool Daily Courier.*

Mrs. LAUDER has made a collection of every species of tale, supernatural or not, long or short, which can in any way be attached to the Harz Mountains. Some are undoubtedly legends, some are mere anecdotes, and not a few are apparently historical tales of the writer's own invention. . . . The child is to be envied who learns to read from such a collection.—*The Saturday Review.*

This is an excellent book to take up and dip into at moments of ease. Nor will it be enjoyed by boys and girls alone.—*The Academy.*

Is a collection of quaint traditions connected with the district of the Harz. The stories, of course, vary widely in their character. Some are sweet and pleasant, refreshing to the reader as is an oasis in the midst of a rugged forest to the weary traveller ; others are wild and stern, like the region that gave them birth. On the whole, the legends are well told, and the book will while away pleasantly an idle hour.—*Dundee Advertiser.*

These legends are told briefly and simply. Some of them are beautiful enough to warrant a few more pages. *Glasgow Herald.*

These legends have the usual Teutonic flavour of the grotesque and sentimental, and they appear to be fairly well done into English. The taste for this kind of literature is an acquired one, but it exists, and may be indulged with more safety than some other cravings. of the imagination.—*Literary World*.

Probably no district is more celebrated for its legendary associations than the Harz Mountains ; it is not, therefore, surprising that Mrs. LAUDER is able to fill upwards of 250 pages with her translations. The vast plain north of the Mountains has been the scene of countless knightly feuds and battles, and to this fact may be attributed many of the legends that have been handed down from the early ages.—*Cook's Excursionist*.

A collection of stories which are not only interesting in themselves, but valuable as showing the kind of romances that are current in the region to which the book relates. The stories are all short, and they are all good—good, that is to say, in the sense that they all have something to tell, and tell it well. Many of them are of a ghostly character, and are marked by a good deal of simplicity of narrative.—*Edinburgh Scotsman*.

Containing about seventy narratives of the class known as *Sagen*, being for the most part traditions which are not wrought out into the dramatic form of fairy tales, but are rather the crude materials of such compositions. The myths of the Kyffhäuser of Princess Ilse, and of the White Lady of Orlamünd, are included in the volume. There is no preface, so that the source whence the stories are derived is not communicated to the reader, an omission which should be made good in any future issue.—*Church Times*.

Lovers of old German stories will thank "TOOFIE LAUDER" heartily for having collected together so charming a volume of "Legends and Tales of the Harz Mountains." Whether the name "TOOFIE LAUDER" signifies a lady or a gentleman, we have no means of guessing, but we should fancy that the graceful style of the book comes from a woman's pen.—*Contemporary Literature*.

"Alone" is an exquisite little poem, woven out of the *true stuff*, and put into the mouth of the broken-hearted young widow whose husband has fallen in the late war with France.—*Schellwien, poet and philosopher*.

I am proud to see our beautiful legends of Germany honoured by so elegant a translation into the English language.—*George Ebers, the celebrated writer of "Egyptian Tales," &c.*

There is not much soul-selling in this collection of legends; and the only case in which a diabolical compact occurs is that of an unfortunate man who, unlike Faust with his lease of life and pleasure, disappears immediately after the fulfilment of his first and only wish. The victim is a monk lying under sentence of death. . . . . . If, however, there are not many stories of the Faust type in the "Legends and Tales of the Harz Mountains," they abound in mystery of one kind or another; and most of them contain something about love. But young ladies are won without the winner having to atone for his success in the world below; and as a rule the persons who have dealings with the supernatural are the better, not the worse for it. . . . The legends are told, for the most part, in a page or two—some in even less space; and the work is written in a simple style which in tales of a mournful character lends itself readily to pathos.—*St. James Gazette.*

This book contains a collection of delightful old legends and folk-lore stories, connected with the wildest and most romantic mountains of Germany. They are full of literary and poetic beauty, and cannot fail to interest both old and young. Some are of an historical nature, others mythical, and so old that their origin is lost in the mist of ages. They read like poems of the infant world. The Legend of the Rosstrappe and Brünhilda is of this class. The Legend of the Golden Crown relates to the recovery of Brünhilda's crown. Charlotte of Blankenburg, in its strange and wonderful incidents, surpasses the fictitious plots of the novels of the day. Eva von Trotta is another historical tale, and is deeply interesting. The mythic legends especially will be read with pleasure by every lover of folk-lore. We would like to take them one by one and give our readers an explanatory analysis of them, but space will not permit. We cannot, however, refrain from saying a few words concerning one of the most delightful stories in the book, that of Princess Ilse. . . . What follows is beautifully told. . . . "The moon rose, and the stars appeared one after another in the dark-blue heavens; fair Ilse chatted on." . . . . In conclusion, we should say that this volume will be read with pleasure by both old and young, and that it will make an excellent gift book.—*St. John's Daily Telegraph.*

. . Further, the legends have been given with great fidelity and beauty, and I wish the fascinating book a brilliant success, not only because of the great amount of study and labour required in the preparation of such a work, but also for its high merits.—*Gustav Freytag, the widely-known German author.*

. . According to MRS. LAUDER, another version of the legend makes the Wild Huntsman the god Woden of the Norse mythology. But on the introduction of Christianity he becomes the Foul Fiend, then the godless hunter, and finally the Wandering Jew. Only on Christmas night may he rest in his unending flight, and then only when he can find a plough in the field on which he may sit down.

. . . A contribution to Canadian literature we will consider it, though written in Germany, published by a London house, and dedicated to Queen Margherita, of Italy. It will afford charming reading for the holidays.—*W. H. Withrow, author of " The Catacombs of Rome."*

It might truly be called an international work, seeing the *stuff* is German, the writer English, and it is dedicated to an Italian Queen.—*German Criticisms.*

EVERGREEN LEAVES;

OR,

TOOFIE IN EUROPE.

BY

MRS. MARIA ELISE T. T. LAUDER.

"A pleasant, chatty description of a lengthened tour through Great Britain and Wales."

BOOKS

PUBLISHED BY

WILLIAM BRIGGS,

78 & 80 KING STREET EAST,

TORONTO.

By the Rev. John Lathern, D.D.

The Macedonian Cry. A Voice from the Lands of Brahma and Buddha, Africa and Isles of the Sea, and A Plea for Missions. 12mo, cloth $0 70

The Hon. Judge Wilmot, late Lieut.-Governor of New Brunswick. A Biographical Sketch. Introduction by the Rev. D. D. Currie. With Artotype portrait. Clo., 12mo. 0 75

Baptisma. Exegetical and Controversial. Cloth, 12mo.... 0 75

By the Rev. E. Barrass, M.A.

Smiles and Tears; or, Sketches from Real Life. With Introduction by the Rev. W. H. Withrow, D.D. Bound in cloth, gilt edges, extra gilt 0 50

By the Rev. J. Cynddylan Jones.

Studies in Matthew. 12mo, cloth. (Canadian Copyright Edition) 1 25

"This is a remarkable volume of Sermons. The style, while severly logical, reminds us in its beauty and simplicity of Ruskin. These are models of what pulpit discourses ought to be."—*Methodist Recorder.*

Studies in Acts. 12mo, cloth........................... 1 50

"No exaggeration to say that Mr. Jones is fully equal to Robertson at his best, and not seldom superior to him."—*Methodist Recorder.*

Studies in Gospel of St. John. 12mo, cloth 1 50

By the Rev. J. Jackson Wray.

Honest John Stallibrass. Illustrated, 12mo, cloth $1 00
Matthew Mellowdew; A Story with More Heroes than One.
Illustrated. Cloth, $1.00. Extra gilt 1 25

"In Matthew Mellowdew, the advantages and happiness of leading a Christian life are urged in an earnest and affecting style."—*Irish Times.*

Paul Meggit's Delusion. Illustrated. Cloth $1 00

"A strong and heartily-written tale, conveying sound moral and religious lessons in an unobjectionable form."—*Graphic.*

Nestleton Magna; A Story of Yorkshire Methodism. Illustrated. Cloth 1 00

"No one can read it without feeling better for its happy simple piety; full of vivacity, and racy of the genuine vernacular of the District."—*Watchman.*

By the Rev. W. H. Withrow, D.D., F.R.S.C

Canadian in Europe. Being Sketches of Travel in France, Italy, Switzerland, Germany, Holland, Belgium, Great Britain and Ireland. Illustrated. Cloth, 12mo 1 25
"Valeria," the Martyr of the Catacombs. A Tale of Early Christian Life in Rome. Illustrated. Cloth 0 75

"The subject is skillfully handled, and the lesson it conveys is noble and encouraging."—*Daily Chronicle.*
"A vivid and realistic picture of the times of the persecution of the Early Christians under Diocletian."—*Watchman.*
"The Story is fascinatingly told, and conveys a vast amount of information."—*The Witness.*

King's Messenger; or, Lawrence Temple's Probation. 12mo, cloth 0 75

"A capital story. . . We have seldom read a work of this kind with more interest, or one that we could recommend with greater confidence."—*Bible Christian Magazine.*

Neville Trueman, the Pioneer Preacher. A Tale of the War of 1812. 12mo, cloth. Illustrated 0 75
Methodist Worthies. Cloth, 12mo, 165 pp............... 0 60
Romance of Missions. Cloth, 12mo, 160 pp 0 60
Great Preachers. Ancient and Modern. Cloth, 12mo 0 60
Intemperance; Its Evils and their Remedies. Paper 0 15
Is Alcohol Food? Paper, 5c., per hundred.. . ... 3 00
Prohibition the Duty of the Hour. Paper, 5c., per hundred . 3 00
The Bible and the Temperance Question. Paper 0 10
The Liquor Traffic. Paper 0 05
The Physiological Effects of Alcohol. Paper 0 10
Popular History of Canada. 600 pp., 8vo. Eight Steel Portraits, One Hundred Wood Cuts, and Six Coloured Maps. Sold only by Subscription 3 00

By the Rev. J. S. Evans.

Christian Rewards; or, I. The Everlasting Rewards for Children Workers; II. The Antecedent Millennial Reward for Christian Martyrs. With notes:—1. True Christians may have Self-love but not Selfishness; 2. Evangelical Faith-works; 3. Justification by Faith does not include a Title to Everlasting Reward. 12mo, cloth 0 50

The One Mediator. Selections and Thoughts on the Propitiatory Sacrifice and Intercessions of our Great High-Priest. 12mo, cloth 1 00

By the Rev. Egerton Ryerson, D.D., LL.D.

Loyalists of America and Their Times. 2 Vols., large 8vo, with Portrait. Cloth, $5; half morocco $7 00

Canadian Methodism; Its Epochs and Characteristics. Handsomely bound in extra cloth, with Steel Portrait of the Author. 12mo, cloth, 440 pp 1 25

The Story of My Life. Edited by Rev. Dr. Nelles, Rev. Dr. Potts, and J. George Hodgins, Esq., LL.D. With Steel Portrait and Illustrations. (Sold only by Subscription.) Cloth, $3; sheep 4 00

By the Rev. Wm. Arthur, M.A.

Life of Gideon Ouseley. Cloth 1 00
All are Living. An attempt to Prove that the Soul while Separate from the Body is Consciously Alive. Each, 3c., per hundred 2 00
Did Christ Die for All? Each, 3c.; per hundred 2 00
Free, Full, and Present Salvation. Each, 3c.; per hundred 2 00
Heroes. A Lecture delivered before the Y.M.C.A. in Exeter Hall, London. Each, 5c.; per hundred 3 00
Is the Bible to Lie Under a Ban In India? A Question for Christian Electors. Each, 3c.; per hundred 2 00
May we Hope for a Great Revival. Each, 3c.; per hundred. 2 00
Only Believe. Each, 3c.; per hundred 2 00
The Christian Raised to the Throne of Christ. Each, 3c.; per hundred 2 00
The Conversion of All England. Each, 3c.; per hundred.. 2 00
The Duty of Giving Away a Stated Portion of Your Income. each, 5c.; per hundred 3 00
The Friend whose Years do not Fail. Each, 3c.; per hundred 2 00

3

Books Published by William Briggs,

By the Rev. W. M. Punshon, D.D., LL.D.

Lectures and Sermons. Printed on thick superfine paper, 378 pp., with fine Steel Portrait, and strongly bound in extra fine cloth.................................. $1 00
> This volume contains some of Dr. Punshon's grandest Lectures and Sermons, which have been listened to by tens of thousands who will remember them as brilliant productions from an acknowledged genius.

Canada and its Religious Prospects. Paper 0 05
Memorial Sermons. Containing a Sermon, each, by Drs. Punshon, Gervase Smith, J. W. Lindsay, and A. P. Lowrey. Paper, 25c.; cloth 0 35
Tabor; or, The Class-meeting. A Plea and an Appeal. Paper, each 5c.; per dozen 0 30
The Prodigal Son, Four Discourses on. 87 pages. Paper, cover, 25c.; cloth.................................. 0 35
The Pulpit and the Pew: Their Duties to each other and to God. Two Addresses. Paper cover, 10c.; cloth. 0 45

By the Rev. E. H. Dewart, D.D.

Broken Reeds; or, The Heresies of the Plymouth Brethren. New and enlarged edition.................. 0 10
**High Church Pretentions Disproved; or, Methodism and the Church of England.............................. 0 10
Living Epistles; or, Christ's Witnesses in the World. 12mo, cloth, 288 pp............................... 1 00
> Rev. Dr. A. C. George, in the New York *Christian Advocate*, says:—"These are, without exception, admirable essays, clear, earnest, logical, convincing, practical, and powerful. They are full of valuable suggestions for ministers, teachers, class-leaders, and all others who desire to present and enforce important biblical truths."
> The New York *Observer* says:—"The essays are practical, earnest, and warm, such as ought to do great good, and the one on Christianity and Scepticism is very timely and well put."

Misleading Lights. A Review of Current Antinomian Theories—The Atonement and Justification, 3c.; per dozen 0 30
Songs of Life. A Collection of Original Poems. Cloth 0 75
Spurious Catholicity. A Reply to the Rev. James Roy.... 0 10
The Development of Doctrine. Lecture delivered before the Theological Union, Victoria College............... 0 20
What is Arminianism? with a Brief Sketch of Arminius. By Rev. D. D. Whedon, D.D., LL.D., with Introduction by Dr. Dewart 0 10
**Waymarks; or, Counsels and Encouragements to Penitent Seekers of Salvation, 5c.; per hundred 3 00

4

By the Rev. J. C. Seymour.

The Temperance Battlefield, and How to Gain the Day.
Illustrated. 12mo, cloth $0 65
Voices from the Throne; or, God's Call to Faith and
Obedience. Cloth................................... 0 50

By the Rev. Alex. Sutherland, D.D.

A Summer in Prairie-Land. Notes of Tour through the
North-West Territory. Paper, 40 cts.; cloth 0 70
Erring Through Wine................................... 0 05

By the Rev. George H. Cornish.

Cyclopædia of Methodism in Canada. Containing Historical,
Educational, and Statistical Information, dating from the
beginning of the work in the several Provinces in the
Dominion of Canada, with Portrait and Illustrations.
Cloth, $4.50; sheep.................................... 5 00
Pastor's Record and Pocket Ritual. Russia limp, 75 cents.
Roan, with flap and pocket 0 90

By the Rev. W. J. Hunter, D.D.

The Pleasure Dance and its Relation to Religion and
Morality.. 0 10
Popular Amusements 0 10

By John Ashworth.

Strange Tales from Humble Life. First series. 12mo, 470
pp., cloth 1 00
Strange Tales from Humble Life. Second series, cloth.... 0 45

By the Rev. H. F. Bland.

Soul-Winning. A Course of Four Lectures delivered at Victoria University 0 30
Universal Childhood Drawn to Christ. With an Appendix
containing remarks on the Rev. Dr. Burwash's "Moral
Condition of Childhood." Paper. 0 10

USEFUL BOOKS.

Webster's Unabridged Dictionary, with Supplement. Bound in sheep $12 50

Webster's Unabridged Dictionary, with Supplement and Denison's Index. Bound in sheep 13 50

Worcester's Unabridged Dictionary, with Supplement. Full sheep 11 00

Chambers's Encyclopædia. 10 vols., cloth 25 00
     "   "   10 vols., half morocco, extra.. 50 00

Schaff-Herzog Encyclopædia. 3 vols., cloth 18 00
     "   "   3 vols., sheep 22 50
     "   "   3 vols., half morocco 27 00

Smith's Bible Dictionary. 4 vols., cloth 20 00
     "   "   "   4 vols., sheep 25 00

Smith & Barnum's Bible Dictionary. 8vo, cloth........ 5 00

McClintock & Strong's Biblical, Theological, and Ecclesiastical Cyclopædia.
     10 vols., cloth 50 00
     10 vols., sheep 60 00
     10 vols., half morocco 80 00

Kitto's Biblical Cyclopædia. 3 vols., cloth 12 60

Young's Great Concordance. Cloth 5 00
     "   "   "   Half Russia, net 5 75

Matthew Henry's Commentary. 3 vols., cloth, net 12 00
     "   "   9 vols., cloth, net 15 00

Adam Clarke's Commentary. Latest edition. Edited by Thornley Smith.
     6 vols., cloth.................................... 20 00
     6 vols., sheep 24 00
     6 vols., half morocco 30 00

Adam Clarke's Commentary. Edited by Dr. Curry. Cloth, per vol. 3 00

&c., &c., &c., &c.

All the latest English and American editions of standard and other books kept in stock or got to order promptly. Sunday-school Library and Prize Books in great variety.

WILLIAM BRIGGS,
78 & 80 KING STREET EAST. TORONTO.

C. W. COATES, MONTREAL.   S. F. HUESTIS, HALIFAX, N.S.

ImTheStory.com

Personalized Classic Books in many genre's

Unique gift for kids, partners, friends, colleagues

Customize:

- Character Names
- Upload your own front/back cover images (optional)
- Inscribe a personal message/dedication on the inside page (optional)

Customize many titles Including

- Alice in Wonderland
- Romeo and Juliet
- The Wizard of Oz
- A Christmas Carol
- Dracula
- Dr. Jekyll & Mr. Hyde
- And more...

CPSIA information can be obtained at www.ICGtesting.com
Printed in the USA
LVOW09s0007041114

411901LV00014B/482/P

9 781313 285186